T4-ADI-562

ORACLES ON MAN
AND
GOVERNMENT

MACMILLAN AND CO., Limited
LONDON · BOMBAY · CALCUTTA · MADRAS
MELBOURNE

THE MACMILLAN COMPANY
NEW YORK · BOSTON · CHICAGO
DALLAS · SAN FRANCISCO

THE MACMILLAN CO. OF CANADA, Ltd.
TORONTO

ORACLES ON MAN

AND

GOVERNMENT

BY

JOHN VISCOUNT MORLEY
O.M., P.C.
HONORARY FELLOW OF ALL SOULS COLLEGE, OXFORD

MACMILLAN AND CO., LIMITED
ST. MARTIN'S STREET, LONDON

1923

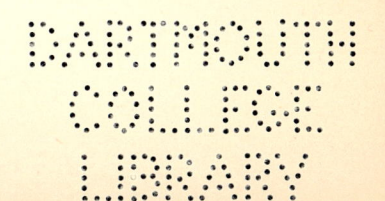

COPYRIGHT

The text of the present edition follows that of the definitive Edition de Luxe of Lord Morley's Works as revised by the author in 1921.

PRINTED IN GREAT BRITAIN

CONTENTS.

	PAGE
A GREAT TEACHER	1
TWO ESSAYS ON DEMOCRACY EXAMINED:	
(I.) LECKY ON DEMOCRACY	29
(II.) MAINE ON POPULAR GOVERNMENT	75
LIBERALISM AND REACTION	115
APHORISMS	153
VAUVENARGUES	187
A FEW WORDS ON FRENCH MODELS	225
AUGUSTE COMTE	251

A GREAT TEACHER.[1]

It was no bad usage of the old Romans to bring down from its niche the waxen image of an eminent ancestor on the anniversary of his natal day, and to recall his memory and its lineaments, even though time with all its wear and tear should have sprinkled a little dust or chipped a feature. Nor was the Alexandrian sage unwise who deemed himself unworthy of a birthday feast, and kept its very date strictly secret, yet sacrificed to the gods and entertained his friends on the birthdays of Socrates and Plato. Nobody would have been more severely displeased than Mill at an attempt to exalt him to a level in the empyrean with those two immortal shades; yet he was of the Socratic household. He was the first guide and inspirer of a generation that has now all but passed away; and it may perhaps be counted among the *sollemnia pietatis*, the feasts and offices of grateful recollection, in an Easter holiday from more clamorous things, to muse for a

[1] Born May 20, 1806; died May 8, 1873. This *causerie* appeared in the *Times*, May 18, 1906. One or two pieces are included from my review of the *Autobiography*.

day upon the teacher who was born on the twentieth of May a hundred years ago.

Mill was once called by Mr. Gladstone the saint of rationalism, and the designation was a happy one. The canonisation of a saint in the Roman communion is preceded by the dozen or more preliminary steps of beatification; and the books tell us that the person to be beatified must be shown to have practised in a signal degree the three theological virtues of Faith, Hope, and Charity, and the four cardinal virtues of Prudence, Justice, Courage, and Temperance. I think Mill would emerge in safety from such an inquisition, on any rational or rationalistic interpretation of those high terms. His life was true to his professions, and was no less tolerant, liberal, unselfish, single-minded, high, and strenuous, than they were.

Nobody who claims to deal, as a matter of history, with the intellectual fermentation between 1840 and 1870 or a little longer, whatever value the historian may choose to set upon its products, can fail to assign a leading influence to Mill. One of the choicest spirits of our age, for example, was Henry Sidgwick, and he has told how he began his study of philosophy with the works of Mill, 'who, I think, had attained the full height (1860) of the remarkable influence he exercised over youthful thought, and perhaps I may say the thought of the country generally, for a period of some years.' ' No one thinker, so far as I know, has ever had anything like equal influence in the forty years or so that have elapsed since Mill's dominion began to weaken.' To dilate on Mill's achievements, said Herbert Spencer, 'and to insist upon the wideness of his influence over the thought of his time, and consequently over the action of his time, seems to me superfluous.' Spencer was rightly chary of random compliments, yet he declared that he should value Mill's agreement more than that of any other thinker. It would be easy to collect copious testimony to this extraordinary supremacy. One may recall Taine's vivacious dialogue with some Oxford friend, actual or imaginary, in the 'sixties:

What have you English got that is original?—Stuart Mill.—What is Stuart Mill?—A publicist: his little book on *Liberty* is as good as your Rousseau's *Social Contract* is bad, for Mill concludes as strongly for the independence of the individual as Rousseau for the despotism of the State.—That is not enough to make a philosopher. What else?—An economist, who goes beyond his science, and subordinates production to man, instead of subordinating man to production.—Still not enough to make a philosopher. What more?—A logician. —Of what school?—His own. I told you he was an original.—Then who are his friends?—Locke and Comte in the front; then Hume and Newton.—Is he systematic? —a speculative reformer?—Oh, he has far too much mind for that. He does not pose in the majesty of a restorer of science; he does not proclaim, like your Germans, that his book is going to open a new era for the human race. He walks step by step, a little slowly, and often close to the ground, across a host of instance and example. He excels in giving precision to an idea, in disentangling a principle, in recovering it from under a crowd of different cases, in refuting, in distinguishing, in arguing.—Has he arrived at any great conception of a Whole?—Yes.—Has he a personal and complete idea of nature and the human mind?—Yes.

Though the reader, if he be so minded, may smile at this to-day, still it is a true summary of the claim then made for Mill, of the position generally assented to (by Taine himself among others), and of aims partially if not wholly achieved. Bentham founded a great school, James Mill inspired a political group, Dugald Stewart impressed a talented band with love of virtue and of truth. John Mill possessed for a time a more general ascendancy than any of these. Just as Macaulay's *Essays* fixed literary and historical subjects for the average reader, so the writings of Mill set the problems and defined the channels for people with a taste for political thinking, and thinking deeper than political. He opened all the ground, touched all the issues, posed all the questions in the spheres where the abstract intellects of men must be most active. It is true, Mill's fame and influence are no longer what they were. How should they be? As if perpetuity of direct power or of personal renown could fall to any philosopher's lot, outside the little group consecrated by tradition. Books outside of the enchanted realm of art and imagination become spent forces; men who were the driving agents of their day sink into literary names, and take a faded place in the catalogue of exhausted influences.

The philosophic teacher's fame, like the statesman's or the soldier's—like the great navigator's, inventor's, or discoverer's—*è color d' erba,* is like the grass, whose varying hue

> Doth come and go—by that same sun destroyed
> From whose warm ray its vigour first it drew.

New needs emerge. Proportions change. Fresh strata are uncovered. Theories once charged with potency evaporate. So a later generation must play umpire. How should Mill be better off than Grotius or Montesquieu, Descartes or Locke, or Jean Jacques, or any of the others who in their day shook the globe, or lighted up some single stage of the world's dim journey? As is well put for our present case, a work great in itself and of exclusive authorship is not the only way in which original power manifests itself. 'A multitude of small impressions,' says Bain, the most sinewy of Mill's allies, 'may have the accumulated effect of a mighty whole. Who shall sum up Mill's collective influence as an instructor in politics, ethics, logic, and metaphysics? No calculus can integrate the innumerable little pulses of knowledge and of thought, that he has made to vibrate in the minds of his generation.'

The amazing story of his education is well known from his own account of it. In after years he told Miss Caroline Fox, whose *Journals* are the most attractive of all the surviving memorials of Mill, 'that his father made him study ecclesiastical history before he was ten. This method of early intense application he would not recommend to others; in most cases it would not answer, and where it does, the buoyancy of youth is entirely superseded by the maturity of manhood, and action is very likely to be merged in reflection. "I never was a boy," he said, "never played at cricket; it is better to let Nature have her own way."' He has told us what were his father's moral inculcations—justice, temperance (to which he gave a very extended application), veracity, perseverance, readiness to encounter pain and especially labour; regard for the public good; estimation of persons according to their merits, and of things according to their intrinsic usefulness; a life of exertion in contradiction to one of self-indulgent ease and sloth. But James Mill, when all was said, 'thought human life a poor thing at best, after the freshness of youth and of satisfied curiosity had gone by.' He would sometimes say that if life were made what it might be by good government and good education, it would be worth having, but he never spoke with anything like enthusiasm even of that possibility. Passionate emotions he regarded as a form of madness, and the intense was a byword of scornful disapprobation. In spite of training, his son grew to be very different. John Mill's opinions on subjects where emotion was possible or appropriate were suffused by feeling; and admiration, anger, contempt often found expression intense enough. Nor did a hint ever escape him about life being 'a poor thing at best.' All pointed the other way. 'Happiness,' he once wrote, 'is not a life of rapture; but moments of such, in an existence made up of few and transitory pains, many and various pleasures, with a decided predominance of the active over the passive, and having as the foundation of the whole not to expect from life more than it is capable of bestowing.' Even friendly philosophers have denounced this as a rash and off-hand formula, and they may be right; for anything that I know, analysis might kill it. Meanwhile it touches at least three vital points in a reasonable standard for a life well laid out. Mill had his moments of discouragement, but they never lasted long and never arrested effort.

He realised how great an expenditure of the reformer's head and heart, to use his own phrase, went in vain attempts to make the political dry bones live. With cheerful stoicism he accepted this law of human things. 'When the end comes,' he wrote to a friend in pensive vein, 'the whole of life will appear but as a day, and the only question of any moment to us then will be, Has that day been wasted? Wasted it has not been by those who have been, for however short a time, a source of happiness and of moral good even to the narrowest circle. But there is only one plain rule of life eternally binding, and independent of all variation of creeds, embracing equally the greatest moralities and the smallest; it is this. Try thyself unweariedly till thou findest the highest thing thou art capable of doing, faculties and circumstances being both duly considered, and then do it.' This responsibility for life and gifts was once put by Gladstone as a threefold disposition : to resist the tyranny of self ; to recognise the rule of duty ; to maintain the supremacy of the higher over the lower parts of our nature. Mill had none of Gladstone's faith in an overruling Providence ; but in a famous passage he set out his conviction that social feeling in men themselves might do as well :

This firm foundation is that of the social feelings of mankind ; the desire to be in unity with our fellow creatures, which is already a powerful principle in human nature, and happily one of those which tend to become stronger, even without express inculcation, from the influences of civilisation. Men are under a necessity of conceiving themselves as at least abstaining from all the grosser injuries, and (if only for their own protection) living in a state of constant protest against them. They are also familiar with the fact of co-operating with others, and proposing to themselves a collective, not an individual, interest, as the aim (at least for the time being) of their actions. . . . Not only does all strengthening of social ties, and all healthy growth of society, give to each individual a stronger personal interest in practically consulting the welfare of others ; it also leads him to identify his feelings more and more with their good, or at least with an ever greater degree of practical consideration for it. He comes, as though instinctively, to be conscious of himself as a being who of course pays regard to others. The good of others becomes to him a thing naturally and necessarily to be attended to, like any of the physical conditions of our existence. . . . In an improving state of mind, the influences are constantly on the increase which tend to generate in each individual a feeling of unity with all the rest; which feeling, if perfect, would make him never think of, or desire, any beneficial condition for himself, in the benefits of which they are not included.

The failure of what he regarded as an expiring theology, made this exaltation of social feeling a necessity. One profound master sentiment with Mill was passionate hatred for abuse of power, either coarse or subtle. Hatred of oppression in all its forms burned deep in his inmost being. It inspired those fierce pages against the maleficence of Nature (in the *Three Essays on Religion*), his almost vindictive indictment of Nature's immorality—immoral because ' the course of natural phenomena is replete with everything that when committed by human beings is most worthy of abhorrence; so that any one who endeavoured in his actions to imitate the natural course of things, would be universally seen and acknowledged to be the wickedest of men.' This poignant piece is perhaps the only chapter to be found in his writings where he throws aside his ordinary measure and reserve, and allows himself the stern relief of vehement and exalted declamation. The same wrath that blazes in him when he is asked to use glozing words about the moral atrocities of Nature to man, breaks out unabated when he recounts the tyrannical brutalities of man to woman. Nor did the flame of his indignation burn low, when he thought of the callous recklessness of men and women to helpless animals—our humble friends and ministers whose power of loyalty, attachment, patience, fidelity, so often seems to deserve as good a word as human, or a better.

The great genius of Pity in that age was Victor Hugo, and a superb genius it was. But in Mill, pity and wrath at the wrong and the stupidities of the world nerved him to steadfast work and thought in definite channels. His postulate of a decided predominance of the active over the passive, meant devotion of thought to practical ends. His life was not stimulated by mere intellectual curiosity, but by the resolute purpose of furthering human improvement. Nor had he the delight that prompts some strong men in dialectic for its own sake; he would have cared as little for this vain eristic, as he cared for the insipid pleasures and spurious business that go to make up the lower species of men of the world. His daily work at the old East India House; vigorous and profitable disputation with a chosen circle of helpful friends; much travelling; lending a hand in reviews or wherever else he saw a way of spreading the light—such were the outer events. In all he was bent on making the most of life as a sacred instrument for good purposes. The production of two such works as the *Logic* (1843) and the *Political Economy* (1848) was drain enough on vital energy. They were the most sustained of his efforts. But he never desisted nor stood still.

He sat in the House of Commons for Westminster

during a short and a bad Parliament (1865-1868), where old parties were at sea, new questions were insincerely handled, and the authority of leaders was dubious and disputable. The oratory happened to be brilliant, but Mill was never of those who make the ideal of government to be that which consists 'in the finest speeches made before the steadiest and largest majority.' Fawcett, the most devoted of all his personal and political adherents, and at that time himself a member, used to insist that Mill's presence in the House was of value as raising the moral tone of that powerful but peculiar assembly. At the same time he could not but deplore the excessive sensitiveness to duty and conscience that made Mill nail himself to his seat from the opening of every sitting to its end. Mill would perhaps have had a better chance of real influence in our more democratic House to-day, than in that hour of unprincipled faction and bewildered strategy. As it was, members felt that his presence was in some way an honour to them, and they listened with creditable respect to speeches that were acute, well argued, apt for the occasion, and not too long nor too many. But, after all, Mill was not of them, and he was not at home with them. Bright, when privately reproached for dissenting on the ballot or something else from so great a thinker, replied in his gruffest tone that the worst of great thinkers is that they generally think wrong. The sally would have been ungrateful if it had been serious, for on all the grand decisive issues—American Slavery, Free Trade, Reform—Mill and Bright fought side by side. He was sometimes spoken of for the India Office when the time should come, and he undoubtedly knew more of India than all Secretaries of State ever installed there put together. But he had refused a seat on the Indian Council when it was first formed, for the reason that he doubted the working of the new system; and as it happened, he lost his seat in Parliament before the Liberals returned to power (when, by the way, India was proposed to Bright). So we cannot test Mill by the old Greek saw that office shows the man. His true ambition, and a lofty one it must be counted, was to affect the course of events in his time by affecting the course of thought.

It is a curious irony that the author of the inspiring passage on Social Feeling, above quoted, should be a target for slings and arrows from Socialist sects, as the cold apostle of hardened individualism. As if the obnoxious creed in this, its narrow sense, were in those days possible to any reflective mind of Mill's calibre. The terrific military surge that swept and roared over Europe for a quarter of a century after the fall of the French monarchy in 1789, no sooner drew back from the shore than there emerged what we summarily style the Social Question. Catholic writers of marked grasp and vision entered upon the field of social reconstruction with Conservative sword and trowel in their hands, to be followed in due time by champions from within the same fold, and aiming at the same reconciliation, but armed with the antagonistic principles of Liberalism. In England Bentham and his school applied themselves to social reform, mainly in the sphere of law, with the aid of democratic politics. All that was best and soundest in Benthamism was absorbed by Mill. He widened its base, deepened the philosophic foundations, and in his *Logic* devised an approach to reform from a novel direction, far away from platforms, Cabinets, bills, and electioneering posters. ' The notion,' he says in his *Autobiography*, ' that truths external to the mind may be known by intuition or consciousness, independently of observation or experience, is, I am persuaded, in these times, the great intellectual support of false doctrines and bad institutions. By the aid of this theory every inveterate belief and every intense feeling, of which the origin is not remembered, is enabled to dispense with the obligation of justifying itself by reason, and is erected into its own all-sufficient voucher and justification. There never was such an instrument devised for consecrating all deep-seated prejudices.' The *Logic* was an elaborate attempt to perform the practical task of dislodging intuitive philosophy, as a step towards sounder thinking about society and institutions; as a step, in other words, towards Liberalism.

In 1861 Taine wrote a chapter on the book, and Mill said no more exact or complete idea of its contents as a body of philosophic doctrine could be found. But he demurred to Taine's description of its psychology as peculiarly English, and Mill's words give an interesting glimpse of his own view of his place in the filiation of philosophy. The psychology was peculiarly English, he says, in the first half of the eighteenth century, beginning with Locke down to the reaction against Hume. This reaction, beginning in Scotland, long dressed itself in German form, and ended by invading the whole field. 'When I wrote my book, I stood nearly alone in my opinion; and though my way of looking at matters found a degree of sympathy that I did not expect, there were still to be found in England twenty *a priori* and spiritualist philosophers for one partisan of the doctrine of experience. Throughout the whole of our reaction of seventy years, the philosophy of experience has been regarded as French, just as you qualify it as English. Each view is a mistake. The two systems follow each other by law of reaction all over the world. Only the different countries never exactly coincide either in revolution or counter-revolution.'

There is no room here to state, discuss, estimate, or classify Mill's place in the stream of philosophic history. The volume of criticism to which he exposed such extensive surface was immense, and soon after his death the hostile tide began pretty rapidly to rise. T. H. Green, at the height of his influence in Oxford, assailed Mill's main positions both in logic and metaphysic. Dr. Caird urged fresh objections. They multiplied. It was inevitable that they should. Those later writings of his which brought Mill's vogue to a climax, appeared at the very moment when there broke upon the scene those overwhelming floods of evolutionary speculation, which seemed destined to shift or sweep away the beacons that had lighted his philosophic course. *Liberty*, for instance, was published in 1859, the very year of Darwin's *Origin of Species*. As one of the most ardent disciples of the school has put the matter in slightly excited form—when the new progressive theories burst upon the world, Comte was left stranded, Hegel was relegated with a bow to a few Oxford tutors, Buckle was exploded like an inflated wind-bag, and 'even Mill himself—*clarum et venerabile nomen*—was felt to be lacking in full appreciation of the dynamic and kinetic element in universal nature.' Mill has not been left without defenders. One of them (Mr. Hobhouse) holds that the head and front of his offending was that, unlike other philosophers, he wrote intelligibly enough for inconsistencies to be found out. Mr. Haldane, who regards the *Examination of Hamilton* as the greatest of Mill's writings, vindicates a place for him as going far down in the deepest regions of ontology, as coming near to the old conclusions of the Germans long ago, 'conclusions to which many writers and thinkers of our time are now tending.' The third book of the *Logic* (on

Induction) is counted by competent judges to be the best work he ever did. So far, the most elaborate exposition, criticism, and amplification of Mill's work and thought has come from the brave and true-hearted Leslie Stephen in one of his volumes on the Utilitarians.

Whether Mill tried to pass ' by a highway in the air ' from psychological hedonism to utilitarianism; whether his explanation of the sentence, ' The Marshal Niel is a yellow rose,' be right or wrong; whether the basis on which he founds induction be strong or weak; whether his denial of the accuracy of geometry has or has not a real foundation; whether his doctrine of ' inseparable association ' exposes the radical defect in the laws of association—these, and the hundred other questions over which expert criticism has ranged ever since his time, are not for us to-day. Even those who do not place him highest, agree that at least he raised the true points, put the sharpest questions, and swept away the most tiresome cobwebs. If the metaphysical controversy has not always been good-natured, perhaps it is because *on ne se passionne que pour ce qui est obscur.*

In point of literary style—a thing on which many coxcombries have sprung up since Mill's day— although both his topics and his temperament denied him a place among the greatest masters, yet his writing had for the younger men of his generation a grave power well fitted for the noble task of making men love truth and seek it. There is no ambition in his style. He never forced his phrase. Even when anger moves him, the ground does not tremble, as when Bossuet or Burke exhorts, denounces, wrestles, menaces, and thunders. He has none of the incomparably winning graces by which Newman made mere siren style do duty for exact, penetrating, and coherent thought; by which, moreover, he actually raised his Church to what would, not so long before, have seemed a strange and incredible rank in the mind of Protestant England. Style has worked many a miracle before now, but none more wonderful than Newman's. Mill's journey from Bentham, Malthus, Ricardo, to Coleridge, Wordsworth, Comte, and then on at last to some of those Manichean speculations that so perplexed or scandalised his disciples, was almost as striking, though not so picturesquely described, as Newman's journey from Evangelicalism to Rome. He did not impose; he drew, he led, he quickened with a living force and fire the commonplace that truth is a really serious and rather difficult affair, worth persistently pursuing in every path where duty beckons. He made people feel, with a kind of eagerness evidently springing from internal inspiration, that the true dignity of man is mind.

We English have never adopted the French word *justesse*, as distinct from justice; possibly we have been apt to fall short in the quality that *justesse* denotes. 'Without *justesse* of mind,' said Voltaire, 'there is nothing.' If we were bound to the extremely unreasonable task of finding a single word for a mind so wide as Mill's in the range of its interests, so diversified in methods of intellectual approach, so hospitable to new intellectual and moral impressions, we might do worse than single out *justesse* as the key to his method, the key to what is best in his influence, the master mark and distinction of his way of offering his thoughts to the world. Measure and reserve in mere language was not the secret, though neither teacher nor disciple can be the worse for measuring language. In a country where, as has often been said, politics and religion are the two absorbing fields of discussion, and where politics is the field in which men and newspapers are most incessantly vocal and vociferous, *justesse* naturally seems but a tame and shambling virtue. For if we were always candid, always on the watch against over-statement, always anxious to be even fairer to our adversary's case than to our own, what would become of politics? Why, there would be no politics. In that sphere we must, as it might seem, accept the dictum of Dr. Johnson, that ' to treat your opponent with respect is to give him an advantage to which he is not entitled.'

If it be true that very often more depends upon the temper and spirit in which men hold their opinions than upon the opinions themselves, Mill was indeed our benefactor. From beginning to end of his career he was forced into the polemical attitude over the whole field; into an incessant and manful wrestle for what he thought true and right against what he regarded as false or wrong. One of his merits was the way in which he fought these battles—the pains he took to find out the strength of an opposing argument; the modesty that made him treat the opponent as an equal; an entire freedom from pedagogue's arrogance. In one or two of his earlier pieces he knows how to give a trouncing; to Brougham, for instance, for his views on the French Revolution of 1848. His private judgments on philosophic or other performances were often severe. Dean Mansel preached a once celebrated set of Bampton lectures against him, and undergraduates flocked to Saint Mary's to hear them, with as much zest as they would to-day manifest about fiscal reform or the Education Bill. Mill privately spoke of Mansel's book as 'loathsome,' but his disdain was usually mute. A philosopher once thought that a review of his theory of vision was arrogant and overbearing. Mill replied in words that are a good example of his canons for a critic:

We are not aware of any other arrogance than is implied by thinking ourselves right and by consequence Mr. Bailey wrong. We certainly did not feel ourselves required, by consideration for him, to state our difference of opinion with pretended hesitation. We should not have written on the subject unless we had been able to form a decided opinion on it, and having done so, to have expressed that opinion otherwise than decidedly would have been cowardice, not modesty; it would have been sacrificing our conviction of truth to fear of offence. To dispute the soundness of a man's doctrines and the conclusiveness of his arguments may always be interpreted as an assumption of superiority over him; true courtesy, however, between thinkers is not shown by refraining from this sort of assumption, but by tolerating it in one another.

It was this candid, patient, and self-controlled temper that provoked the truly remarkable result—a man immersed in unsparing controversy for most of his life (controversy, too, on all the subjects where difference of opinion is aptest to kindle anger, contempt, and even the horrid and irrelevant imputation of personal sin), and yet somehow held in general honour as a sort of oracle, instead of having presented to him the fatal cup of hemlock that has so often been the reformer's portion. He really succeeded in procuring a sort of popular halo round the dismal and derided name of philosopher, and his books on political theory and sociological laws went into cheap popular editions. Like Locke and Hobbes, he propounded general ideas for particular occasions, and built dykes and ramparts on rational principles for movements that had their source not so much in reasoning in 'the world and waves of men,' as in passions and interests, sectarian or material, and in the confused and turbid rush of intractable events.

Among all the changes of social ordinance in Mill's day and generation, none is more remarkable, and it may by and by be found that none cuts deeper, than the successive stages of the emancipation of women. And to this no thinker or writer of his time contributed so powerfully as Mill. Much of the ground has now been won, but the mark made by his little tract on the *Subjection of Women* upon people of better minds among us was profound, and a book touching so impressively the most penetrating of all our human relations with one another is slow to go quite out of date.

In political economy (1848) he is admitted, by critics not at all disposed to put his pretensions too high, to have exercised without doubt a greater influence than any other writer since Ricardo, and as an exposition of the principles on which the emancipating work between 1820 and 1860 was done, his book still holds its ground. Without being tempted into the controversies of the fugitive hour, it is enough to mark that Mill is not of those economists who treat their propositions as absolute and dogmatic, rather than relative and conditional, depending on social time and place. One of the objects that he always had most at heart, in his capacity as publicist, was to set democracy on its guard against itself. No object could be either more laudable or more needed. He was less successful in dealing with Parliamentary machinery than in the infinitely more important task of moulding and elevating popular character, motives, ideals, and steady respect for truth, equity, and common sense—things that matter a vast deal more than machinery. Save the individual; cherish his freedom; respect his growth and leave room for it—this was ever the refrain. His book on Representative Government set up the case against Carlyle's glorification of men like Napoleon or Frederick. Within twenty years from Mill's death the tide had turned Carlyle's way, and now to-day it has turned back again. Then in the ten years before his death Neo-machiavellianism rose to ascendancy on the Continent of Europe, and a quarter of a century later we have had a short spell of Neo-machiavellianism in England—end justifying means, country right or wrong, and all the rest of it (1906). Here again the tide has now turned, and Millite sanity might for a new season be restored. In the sovereign field of tolerance his victory has been complete. Only those who can recall the social odium that surrounded heretical opinions before Mill began to achieve popularity, are able rightly to appreciate the battle in which he was in so many aspects the protagonist.

Mill's life as disclosed to us in his *Autobiography* has been called joyless, by that sect of religious partisans whose peculiarity is to mistake boisterousness for unction. Can the life of any man be joyful who sees and feels the tragic miseries and hardly less tragic follies of the earth? The old Preacher, when he considered all the oppressions that are done under the sun, and beheld the tears of such as were oppressed and had no comforter, therefore praised the dead which are already dead more than the living which are yet alive, and declared him better than both, who hath not yet been, who hath not seen the evil work that is done under the sun. Those who are willing to play fast and loose with words may, if they please, console themselves with the commonplaces of a philosophic optimism. They may, with eyes tight shut, cling to the notion that they live in the best of all possible worlds, or, discerning all the anguish that may be compressed into threescore years and ten, still try to accept the Stoic's paradox that pain is not an evil.

Mill's conception of happiness is more intelligible if we contrast it with his father's. The Cynic element in James Mill, as his son tells us (p. 48), was that he had scarcely any belief in pleasures; he thought few of them worth the price which has to be paid for them; and he set down the greater number of the miscarriages in life as due to an excessive estimate of them. We should shrink from calling even this theory dreary, associated as it is with the rigorous enforcement of the heroic virtues of temperance and moderation, and the strenuous bracing up of every faculty to face the inevitable and make the best of it. We can have no difficulty in understanding that, when the elder Mill lay dying, 'his interest in all things and persons that had interested him through life was undiminished, nor did the approach of death cause the smallest wavering (as in so strong and firm a mind it was impossible that it should), in his convictions on the subject of religion. His principal satisfaction, after he knew that his end was near, seemed to be the thought of what he had done to make the world better than he found it; and his chief regret in not living longer, that he had not had time to do more ' (p. 203).[1]

J. S. Mill, however, went beyond this conception. He had a belief in pleasures, and thought human life by no means a poor thing to those who know how to make the best of it. It was essential both to his utilitarian philosophy, and to the contentment of his own temperament, that the reality of happiness should be vindicated. He did both vindicate and attain it. A highly pleasurable excitement that should have no end, of course he did not think possible; but he regarded the two constituents of a satisfied life, much tranquillity combined with some excitement, as perfectly attainable by many men, and as ultimately attainable by very many more. The ingredients of this satisfaction he set forth as follows:—a willingness not to expect more from life than life is capable of bestowing; an intelligent interest in the objects of mental culture; genuine private affections; and a sincere interest in the public good. What, on the other hand, are the hindrances that prevent these elements from being in the possession of every one born in a civilised country? Ignorance; bad laws or customs,

[1] For the mood in which death was faced by another person who had renounced theology and the doctrine of a future state of consciousness, see Miss Martineau's *Autobiography*, ii. 435, etc.

debarring a man or woman from the sources of happiness within reach; and 'the positive evils of life, the great sources of physical and mental suffering—such as indigence, disease, and the unkindness, worthlessness, or premature loss of objects of affection.'[1] But every one of these calamitous impediments is susceptible of the weightiest modification, and some of them of final removal. Mill had learnt from Turgot and Condorcet, among many other lessons, this of the boundless improvableness of the human lot, and we may believe that he read over many a time the pages in which Condorcet delineated the Tenth Epoch in the history of human perfectibility, and traced out in words of reserved enthusiasm the operation of the forces that should consummate the progress of the race. 'All the grand sources of human suffering,' Mill thought, ' are in a great degree, many of them almost entirely, conquerable by human care and effort; and though their removal is grievously slow—though a long succession of generations will perish in the breach before the conquest is completed, and this world becomes all that, if will and knowledge were not wanting, it might easily be made—yet every mind sufficiently intelligent and generous to bear a part, however small and unconspicuous, in the endeavour, will draw a noble enjoyment from the contest itself, which he would not for any bribe in the form of selfish indulgence consent to be without' (*Utilitarianism*, 22).

[1] For this exposition see *Utilitarianism*, pp. 18-24.

We thus see how far from dreary this wise and benignant man actually found his own life; how full it was of cheerfulness and animation.

Much has been said against Mill's strictures on society, and his withdrawal from it. If we realise the full force of all that he says of his own purpose in life, it is hard to see how either his opinion or his practice could have been different. He ceased to be content with 'seconding the superficial improvements' in common ways of thinking, and saw the necessity of working at a fundamental reconstitution of accepted modes of thought. This in itself implies a condemnation of a social intercourse that rests on the base of conventional ways of looking at things. The better kind of society, it is true, appears to contain two classes; not only the class that will hear nothing said hostile to the greater social conventions, including among these the popular theology, but also another class who will tolerate or even encourage attack on the greater social conventions, and a certain mild discussion of improvements in them—provided only neither attack nor discussion be conducted in too serious a vein. A new idea about a Supreme Being, or property, or the family, is handed round among the company, as ladies of quality in Queen Anne's time handed round a black page or a China monster. In Bishop Butler's phrase, these people only want to know what is said, not what is true.

In the later years, when he had travelled over

the smooth places of a man's life and the rough places, his younger friends never heard a word fall from him that did not encourage and direct; and nobody that ever lived enjoyed more of that highest of pleasures, the pointing the right path for new wayfarers, urging them to walk in it. 'Montesquieu must die,' exclaimed old Bentham, in a rare mood of rhapsody; 'he must die as his great countryman, Descartes, had died before him: he must wither as the blade withers when the corn is ripe; he must die, but let tears of gratitude and admiration bedew his grave.' So the pilgrim may feel to-day, as he stands by that mournful grave at windy Avignon, city of sombre history and forlorn memories, where Mill's remains were laid a generation ago this month (May 1873). Measure the permanence of his contribution to thought or social action as we will, he will long deserve to be commemorated as the personification of some of the noblest and most fruitful qualities within the reach and compass of mankind.

LECKY ON DEMOCRACY.[1]

WHAT is Democracy? Sometimes it is the name for a form of government by which the ultimate control of the machinery of government is committed to a numerical majority of the community. Sometimes, and incorrectly, it is used to denote the numerical majority itself, the poor or the multitude existing in a state. Sometimes, and still more loosely, it is the name for a policy directed exclusively or mainly to the advantage of the labouring class. Finally, in its broadest, deepest, most comprehensive, and most interesting sense, Democracy is the name for a certain general condition of society, having historic origins, springing from circumstances and the nature of things; not only involving the political doctrine of popular sovereignty, but representing a cognate group of corresponding tendencies over the whole field of moral, social, and even of spiritual life within the democratic community. Few writers have consistently respected the frontier that divides democracy as a certain state of society,

[1] *Democracy and Liberty.* By W. E. H. Lecky. Two vols. Longmans, 1896.

from democracy as a certain form of government. Mill said of the admirable Tocqueville, for instance, that he was apt to ascribe to Democracy consequences that really flowed from Civilisation. Mr. Lecky is constantly open to the same criticism.

Whether we think of democracy in the narrower or the wider sense—whether as another name for universal suffrage, or as another name for a particular stage of civilisation—it equally stands for a remarkable revolution in human affairs. In either sense it offers a series of moral and political questions of the highest practical importance and the most invigorating theoretical interest. It has shaken the strength and altered the attitude of the churches, has affected the old subjection of women and modified the old conceptions of the family and of property, has exalted labour, has created and dominated the huge enginery of the Press, has penetrated in a thousand subtle ways into the whole region of rights, duties, human relations, and social opportunity. In vain have men sought a single common principle for this vast movement. Simplification of life; the sovereignty of the people, and the protection of a community by itself; the career open to the talents; equality and brotherhood; the substitution of industrialism for militarism; respect for labour:—such are some of the attempts that have been made to seize in a phrase the animating spirit of the profound changes through which the civilised world has for a century and more been passing, not only in the imposing institutions of the external world, but in the mind and heart of individual man.

We can hardly imagine a finer or more engaging, inspiring, and elevating subject for inquiry, than this wonderful outcome of the extraordinary industrial, intellectual, and moral development that has awakened in the masses of modern society the consciousness of their own strength, and the resolution, still dim and torpid, but certain to expand and to intensify, to use that strength for new purposes of their own. We may rejoice in democracy, or we may dread it. Whether we like it or detest it, and whether a writer chooses to look at it as a whole or to investigate some particular aspect of it, the examination ought to take us into the highest region of political thought, and it undoubtedly calls for the best qualities of philosophic statesmanship and vision.

If so much may be said of the theme, what of the season and the hour? In our own country, at any rate, the present would seem to be a singularly propitious time for the cool and scientific consideration, by a man trained in habits of systematic reflection, of some of the questions raised by Mr. Lecky's title. The English electorate has called a halt to all projects of constitutional reform. The great orator and statesman who has for a generation been the organ and inspirer of popular sentiment in this kingdom, has quitted the stage of public activity. Of the two historic political parties, though one is for the moment entrenched behind a strong parliamentary majority, yet neither feels perfectly secure against deep internal transformation, nor perfectly easy about the direction which that transformation may take. Victors and vanquished alike ostentatiously proclaim their supreme devotion to the cause of social reform, though the phrase is vague and its contents uncertain and indefinite. The extreme wing of what styles itself the Labour party, the Socialist party, or the Collectivist party, has for the hour suffered a signal repulse. Yet nobody with an eye in his head believes that the accommodation of old social institutions to a state of society in which the political centre of gravity has finally shifted, is a completed task, or that the gravest problems involved in that task are not left outstanding and inexorable.

Such a period as this is just the time, one would think, for a political philosopher to take stock of institutions; to trace their real working under the surface of external forms; to watch for subtle subterranean changes, to classify tendencies, to consider outlying or approaching difficulties, to seek solutions, and to do all these things with as much precision, directness, definiteness, as the highly complex nature of the subject will permit. Precision and directness are not at all the same thing as dogma. As Tocqueville has well said, the books that have done most to make men reflect, and have had most influence on their opinions and their acts, are those where the author has not thought of telling them dogmatically what they ought to think, but where he has set their minds on the road that leads to the truths in point, and has made them find such truths as if by their own effort.

If the theme is lofty, and the hour favourable, what of our teacher? Mr. Lecky has been removed from the distractions of active life, and though this has on the one hand the drawback of keeping him ignorant of many of the vital realities of his subject, it might on the other hand have been expected at least to keep him free from its passions. He has large stores of knowledge of other times and other countries, and he has been accustomed to expatiate upon the facts so accumulated, in copious and impartial dissertations. He might seem to be justified in his belief that studies of this sort bring with them kinds of knowledge, and methods of reasoning, 'that may be of some use in the discussion of contemporary questions.' In other fields he has shown qualities of eminent distinction. From him, if from any living writer, we should have expected firm grasp of his great subject, unity of argument, reflective originality, power, depth, ingenuity; above all, the philosophic temper. In every one of these anticipations it is melancholy to have to say that deep disappointment awaits the reader.

First of all, a word or two as to the form. Mr. Lecky has never been remarkable for skill in handling masses of material. Compare him, for instance, with

Montesquieu: he will admit that the thought of the comparison is not uncomplimentary. Montesquieu subordinates the exposition of facts to the generalisation; detail and generalisation are firmly welded together; illustration never obscures nor blocks the central idea; two or three energetic strokes of the brush bring a mass of fact into true colour, light, and relation; in short, Montesquieu is a master of the art of composition. In these volumes it is very different. Great quantities of fact are constantly getting into the way of the argument, and the importation of history breaks the thread of discussion. The contents of an industrious man's note-books are tumbled headlong down, like coals into the hold of a Tyne collier. I hesitate to pronounce these great quantities of fact irrelevant, because it is not easy to disentangle the author's thesis, to detect his general point of view, or to find a clue through the labyrinth of promiscuous topic and the jungle of overgrown detail. It is impossible to be sure what is relevant and what is not. With the best will in the world, and after attentive and respectful perusal, we leave off with no firm and clear idea what the book is about, what the author is driving at, nor what is the thread of thought that binds together the dozen or score pamphlets, monographs, or encyclopædic articles of which the work is composed. Organic unity is wholly absent; it is a book that is no book. You might as well hunt for the leading principle of what is known in parliamentary speech as an Omnibus Bill. There is a pamphlet of forty pages on that novel and refreshing theme, the Irish Land Question. Thirty pages are filled with the minutiæ of Local Veto. Five-and-forty pages go to the group of questions relating to the Marriage law: we have Roman concubinatus, early Christian marriage, the action of the Council of Trent, the case of Lord Northampton in the time of Edward the Sixth, and so forth through all the ages, down to the deceased wife's sister of the day in which we live, and the ex-Lord Chancellor who declared that, if marriage with the sister of a deceased wife ever became legal, 'the decadence of England was inevitable,' and that for his part he would rather see 300,000 Frenchmen landed on the English coasts. This immense excursus is in its way highly interesting; it lulls us into a most agreeable forgetfulness both of democracy and of liberty; but when we reach the end of it and recover the high road, we rub our eyes and wonder whither we were bound before being wiled into these sequestered bypaths. Then Sunday legislation covers twenty close pages; the observance of Sunday in the Early Church, the laws of Constantine and Theodosius, observance in the Middle Ages, Sunday under Elizabeth, James, and Charles, the *Book of Sports*, the Puritan Sunday, and so on, almost down to the resolution of the House of Commons, a few weeks since, for the opening of museums on the first day. A distinguished ambassador was once, not very many years ago, directed by his government to forward a report on the Kulturkampf in Germany; he sent home a despatch of fifty pages, and apologised for not being able to bring things down lower than Pope Gregory the Seventh, but promised more by the next mail. Mr. Lecky is almost as regardless as the ambassador of the limitations set by time, space, and a definite purpose to the employment of human knowledge.

Worse than digression is platitude. Simplicity is the most delightful quality in literature, and nothing charms like the naïf. When the simple and the naïf degenerates, it turns to platitude, and that is in writing what insipidity is in the art of the cook, or flatness in a flask of wine. If the reader will begin to collect from these volumes a little anthology or *hortus siccus* of deliverances of this rather vapid family, he will find the number of well-marked specimens rising over the hundred in no time. For instance. 'It is in my opinion an exaggerated thing to prohibit harvest-work in the critical weeks during which the prosperity of the farmer so largely depends on the prompt use of every hour of fine weather.' And when he says of children brought up with excessive strictness in religious families: 'Being taught to aim perpetually at a temperament and an ideal wholly unsuited to their characters, they fail to attain the type of excellence which was well within their reach. The multiplication of unreal duties and the confusion of harmless pleasures with vice, destroy the moral proportion and balance of their natures, and as soon as the restraining hand is withdrawn a complete moral anarchy ensues.' So ' depriving the people of innocent means of enjoyment, and preventing the growth of some of the tastes that do most to civilise them, it has often a distinctly demoralising influence' (ii. 94). Most true; excellent sense; but not startlingly new nor deeply impressive. As Rivarol said of his friend's distich, ' *C'est très bien, mais il y a des longueurs.*'

Digression and platitude, though harmless in themselves, unfortunately tend to bulk. Mr. Lecky's object is not the very broadest, though highly important, being really and in substance not much more than to show the effects of popular government upon the rights of property. For this and the two or three allied or subordinate subjects he takes between nine hundred and a thousand pages. Mill's famous book on Representative Government was not one-third so long. Yet it sufficed for a systematic exploration of the most important part of the ground dealt with in these two volumes, and it left the reader with a body of thoughts and principles which, whether they are impregnable or not, are at any rate direct, definite, and coherent. Maine's attack on Popular Government may not have been a very searching performance, but like Stephen's *Liberty, Equality, and Fraternity*, it was sinewy and athletic; the reader knew where he was, and he came to the end of his journey in three or four hundred pages.

A memorable sermon was preached on Mr. Lecky's text nearly thirty years ago; it was called *Shooting Niagara: and After?* 'A superlative Hebrew conjuror,' cried the preacher, 'spellbinding all the great Lords, great Parties, great Interests of England, leading them by the nose like helpless mesmerised somnambulant cattle,' had just passed the Reform Act of 1867—Lathsword and Scissors of Destiny; Pickleherring and three Parcæ alike being in it. 'Inexpressibly delirious seems to me the puddle of Parliament and Public upon what it calls the Reform measure; that is to say, The calling in of new supplies of blockheadism, gullibility, bribability, amenability to beer and balderdash, by way of amending the woes we have had from our previous supplies of that bad article.' These words would have made a concise and appropriate epigraph for Mr. Lecky's book, and I doubt whether the ordinary reader will carry away with him from this book much more than from Carlyle's summary damnation of democracy, and canonisation of aristocracy. Yet Carlyle only took fifty pages. But then Carlyle was a carnivore, and Mr. Lecky has been assigned to the slow-browsing tribe of the graminivorous.

If Mr. Lecky's literary method is bad, I fear that his philosophic temper must be called much worse. In our own generation we have all heard the continental ecclesiastic mourning or raging over the perfidies and robberies of the French Republic or the Piedmontese monarchy; the Southern planter swearing at the violation of vested interests which emancipated his negroes; the drone of the dowager or the spinster of the Faubourg Saint-Germain; the amœbean exchange of their wrongs between a couple of Irish landlords in the smoking-room at Harrogate or Pau. These are assuredly no examples for a philosopher. Mr. Lecky might have been expected to think of such a man as the elder Mill. J. S. Mill tells us that his father was the reverse of sanguine as to the results to be expected from reform in any one particular case; but this did not impair the moral support his conversation and his very existence gave to those who were aiming at the same objects, and the encouragement he afforded to the faint-hearted or desponding among them, by the firm confidence he always felt in the power of reason, the general progress of improvement, and the good which individuals could do by judicious effort. And the world has not yet wholly forgotten Mill's striking account of the good effects of his official position at the India House upon his own work as a theoretical reformer of the opinions and institutions of his time.

The occupation [he says] accustomed me to see and hear the difficulties of every course, and the means of obviating them, stated and discussed deliberately with a view to execution; it gave me opportunities of perceiving when public measures and other political facts did not produce the effects which had been expected of them; above all, it was valuable to me by making me, in this portion of my activity, merely one wheel in a machine, the whole of which had to work together. As a speculative writer I should have had no one to consult but myself. But as a secretary conducting political correspondence, I could not issue an order or express an opinion without satisfying various persons very unlike myself that the thing was fit to be done. . . . I became practically conversant with the difficulties of moving bodies of men, the necessities of compromise, the art of sacrificing the non-essential to preserve the essential. I learnt how to obtain the best I could when I could not obtain everything; instead of being indignant or dispirited because I could not have entirely my own way, to be pleased and encouraged when I could have the smallest part of it; and when even that could not be, to bear with complete equanimity the being overruled altogether (*Autobiog.* p. 85).

If the distinguished author of these two volumes had only cultivated this temper; if he had only ever been under the wholesome compulsion of working with other people; if, like Mill, he had forbidden himself to be indignant and dispirited because the heedless world insists on revolving on its own axis instead of on his; he might well have given us a contribution to political thought that should be stimulating, enlightening, and even practically helpful. As it is, we move in an air of pitchy gloom. The British Constitution is plainly worn out. The balance of power within the country has been destroyed. Diseases of a serious character are fast growing in its political life. It is ruled by feeble governments and disintegrated Parliaments and ignorant constituencies. Power has descended to classes who are less intelligent, less scrupulous, more easily deceived. Low motives are acquiring a greater prominence in English politics. Extension of the franchise makes a popular cry, and is so simple that it lies well within the competence of the vulgarest and most ignorant demagogue: it has sprung from a competition for power and popularity between rival factions; the leaders reckon that new voters will vote, for the first time at any rate, for the party which gave them the vote, and 'it is probably no exaggeration to say that calculations of this kind have been the chief motives of all our recent degradations of the suffrage' (i. 60). This genial and charitable explanation, by the way, seems a little summary, when we remember that the most persevering, eloquent, and effective apostle of the 'degradation of the suffrage' in our day was John Bright, as upright and single-minded a citizen as ever adorned a state.

Then to attack university representation is, it would appear, a horrible fatuity. The assailants, says the author, have rarely the excuse of honest ignorance. They are sycophants, who in former ages would have sought by Byzantine flattery to win the favour of an emperor or a prince, and who now declaim on platforms about the inquity of privilege on the one hand, and the matchless wisdom and nobility of the masses on the other. Many of these declaimers, strange to say, are highly cultivated men, who owe to university education all that they are; they stoop, Mr. Lecky tells us, to the rant of the vulgar demagogue in order to attain personal ends of their own. 'I do not think that the respect of honest men will form any large part of their reward'! (i. 25).

Now was ever discontent so unreasonable? Some people might be excused for a little depression, if life were not too short for depression; but Mr. Lecky has no excuse. At what moment in the century was it easier to find balm for his bruised spirit? When were honest men more triumphantly avenged on the Byzantine sycophants? What more can the most self-righteous of pedants or patriots desire than the result of the general election of last July?[1] 'The country had now the opportunity of expressing its opinion about these men, their objects, and their methods, and it gave an answer which no sophistry could disguise and no stupidity could misunderstand. The complete, crushing, and unequivocal defeat of the Radical party in 1895 is certainly one of the most memorable events in the present generation' (i. 362). 'The lesson was a salutary one,' for it proved beyond dispute the profound conservatism of the masses of the English people and their genuine attachment to the institutions of their country. 'It showed how enormously men had overrated the importance of the noisy groups of Socialists, faddists, and revolutionists that float

[1] In the election of 1895 the Liberals, including more than one of their foremost men, were signally routed. They did not regain a majority for ten years.

upon the surface of English political thought like froth-flakes on a deep and silent sea' (i. 363). But is there not a whiff of the Byzantine sycophant here? What has become of the manly and austere words only two hundred pages before (i. 184), about 'canonising and almost idolising mere majorities, even when they are mainly composed of the most ignorant men, voting under all the misleading influences of side-issues and violent class or party passions'? The blessed events of one blithe summer week have happily transformed this mass of ignorant and passionate dupes into a deep and silent sea of innate conservatism and real attachment to the institutions of their country. But what, again, has become of the haughty lines about those contemptible beings to whom 'the voice of the people,' as expressed at the polls, is the sum of all wisdom, the supreme test of truth or falsehood? Nay, 'it is even more than this: it is invested with something very like the spiritual efficacy which theologians have ascribed to baptism. It is supposed to wash away all sin. However unscrupulous, however dishonest, may be the acts of a party or of a statesman, they are considered to be justified beyond reproach if they have been condoned or sanctioned at a general election' (i. 184). Lo, now it seems that one of the most memorable party events of this generation does show that there is really some spiritual efficacy, some baptismal grace, some supreme test of truth and falsehood, in the voice of the people as expressed at the polls, after all.

While our philosopher is thus mercilessly bastinadoing us with his general election, we can only gasp out, between his blows, his own lofty words: 'Of all the forms of idolatry, I know none more irrational or ignoble than this blind worship of mere numbers.' And if it be really true that the noisy groups of Socialists, faddists, and revolutionists are in this country mere froth-flakes on a deep and silent sea of profound conservatism, then one wonders why three-fourths of this book were ever written. For the secret text of the book, in the mind of its author, is not very different from Talleyrand's saying: '*Democracy—what is it but an aristocracy of blackguards?*' If the lesson of the elections was so salutary for the vaulting revolutionary optimist, was it not a little salutary too for the querulous pessimist?

If it were a sign of a capacious or an elevated mind, always to fly for explanations of conduct or opinions which you do not approve, to the baser parts of human nature, Mr. Lecky would, as we see, occupy a very lofty pedestal. There the censor sits, passing magisterial judgments right and left, not merely on the acts—these are open to the world—but on the motives, of the most conspicuous, as of the humblest, men of his time. He pierces the secrets of their hearts; he knows for certain when their ignorance is honest, and when it is dishonest, and it is almost always dishonest; there is no room in his Rhadamanthine nature for considerations of mixed motive; nor for the strange dualism in men that makes them partly good and partly bad, sometimes strong and sometimes weak; nor for thought of the hard alternatives, the grave and divided responsibilities, the critical balancings in sharp emergencies and clouded situations, that press those who meddle with the government of men. All is intelligible, all is discreditable: all is simple, and all is bad. To pretend to believe that manhood suffrage might be a gain to the commonwealth, or that Mr. Lecky's countrymen are fit for self-government, or that a popular constituency is quite as likely to form sound political judgments as a miscellaneous band of Masters of Arts, is to mark yourself either as what has been described as a fool aspiring to be a knave, or else a 'new Jesuit,' an ignoble place-hunter, a trickster merely 'playing a good card in the party game.' As for the adoption of Home Rule by British Liberals, and the monstrous enormity of a court for arbitrating Irish rents— introduced by the great betrayer, 'with uplifted eyes and saintly aspect'—Dante himself could hardly have found word and image to express the depth of Mr. Lecky's reprobation. Even the proposal of 1894 for restoring evicted tenants to their holdings was 'a scandalous instance of political profligacy.' The great Duke of Marlborough overheard a groom riding in front of him, cursing and swearing at his horse. 'Do you know,' he said to a companion by his side, 'I would not have that fellow's temper for all the world.' Not for all the world would one share Mr. Lecky's conviction as to the mean, the corrupt, the gross and selfish motives of all these poor rogues and peasant slaves with whom his imagination mans the political stage.

The dolorous refrain recurs with terrible monotony. In one place the author is arguing the manifold blessings of hereditary aristocracy. A man who is not marked out in any way by his position for parliamentary distinction, he says, is more tempted than those of another class to make sacrifices of principle and character to win the prize, to be more governed by the desire for office or social distinction. The young patrician is less accessible than poorer men to 'the sordid motives that play so large a part in public life' (i. 315). As a matter of fact, has it ever been understood that in the working of governments, either peers or their elder sons or their younger sons or their relatives and connections of every degree of affinity down even to their butlers out of service and cast-off valets—have been wont to show any indifference to the emoluments of office? If one could compare the public money received by patrician ministers during the last hundred and fifty years, or even the last reformed fifty years, with the money received by plebeians, from Burke downwards, would not the first be as a giant mountain to a minute mole-hill? But do sordid motives play a large part in our public life? Where are we to look for them? If they play a large part, they ought to be easily seen. Has there ever been a community in the civilised world where such a vast mass of gratuitous work for public purposes is done—work with no taint whatever of sordid personal object or motive, direct or indirect—as we see done every day of our lives in this island? Parliamentary committees, county councils, municipal councils, schoolboards, boards of guardians, asylum boards, quarter sessions—how singular and how unlucky must have been Mr. Lecky's field of observation, if what strikes him most in all these scenes of social activity is, not the devotion and the public spirit and the sacrifice of time and ease, but the play of sordid motives. In truth, this piece of disparagement, as a contradictory passage elsewhere shows, is a mere bit of thoughtlessness. But then, what is the use of a man being a thinker, if he will not think? Bright once said in a splenetic moment, that the worst of great thinkers is that they generally think wrong. Mr. Lecky is worse still.

Then Mr. Lecky writes as if it were a happy peculiarity of 'the gentlemen' to make these sacrifices. He applauds 'a social condition which assigns to a wealthy class a large circle of necessary duties, and makes the gratuitous discharge of public functions the appanage and sign of dignity' (i. 318). As if this were in any special way the appanage and sign of dignity. As if the great mass of public functions gratuitously discharged were not so discharged by plain homely men, who neither claim nor profess any dignity save that which belongs to the faithful and honourable performance of public duty, whether it be done by cobbler or by duke. What more dignity does a man want, and what more can a man have?

The author has not even the merit of sticking to his text. While he thinks that the more Englishmen are admitted to political power, the worse that power will be exercised, yet at the same time, strange to say, he is persuaded both that the national character is good, and that it is every day growing better. Conspicuous improvement, he allows, has taken place in the decorum and humanity of the bulk of the poor; in the character of their tastes and pleasures; in their enlarged circle of interests; in the spirit of providence, and so forth. 'The skilled artisans in our great towns within the memory of living men have become not only the most energetic, but also one of the most intelligent and orderly elements of English life' (i. 204). Just so; and this is the very element that was admitted to direct political power by the Reform Act of 1867, of which Mr. Lecky thinks so exceedingly ill. What are we to make of his reiterated assurances that since 1867 the governing power has descended to classes less intelligent, less scrupulous, and more easily deceived? If the 'bulk of the poor' are conspicuously improving, and if democracy has placed the decisive or prerogative vote—for this is what it has done—in the hands of one of the most intelligent and orderly elements in our national life, then, how comes it that, in face of all these admissions, Mr. Lecky insists, first, that the ignorance of the electorate is increasing; second, that the electorate is made all the more gullible, bribable, foolish, and incompetent, since the inclusion of these elements; third, that their inclusion is a degradation of the suffrage; and fourth, that their inclusion was not due to any spontaneous desire or demand of the intelligent elements themselves—who, we suppose, wished nothing else than that their betters should make laws for them—but to the factious competition of rival leaders (i. 59) and the vulgarest and most incompetent demagogues? Was there ever such a tissue of incoherence and inconsequence?

The author draws a picture of a kind of men loitering listlessly around the doors of every gin-shop—men who through drunkenness, or idleness, or dishonesty, have failed in the race of life. They are, he says, one of the chief difficulties and dangers of all labour questions. With a low suffrage, they become an important element in many constituencies. Their instinct will be to use the power which is given them for predatory and anarchic purposes (i. 20). But the broken loafer is no novelty in our social system, and any electioneering agent of either party will tell Mr. Lecky that this class in nine cases out of ten is the ardent supporter of Church and Queen, and, so far from being predatory, holds the very strongest views as to the righteousness of publican's compensation, for instance. To count these poor losels as a chief difficulty in labour questions, or as aspiring 'to break up society,' is ludicrous.

Still more remarkable is the following passage :

> It is very doubtful whether the spirit of muncipal and local patriotism was more strongly developed either in ancient Greece, or, during the Middle Ages, in the great towns of Italy and Flanders or along the Baltic, than it now is in Birmingham, or Liverpool, or Manchester. The self-governing qualities that are displayed in these great centres, the munificence and patriotism with which their public institutions are supported, the strong stream of distinctive political tendency that emanates from them, are among the most remarkable and most consolatory facts of English life (i. 208).

The very facts that bring this consolation for the Sorrows of our political Werther, are facts showing that he has no ground for being a Werther at all. A town-councillor (with some qualifications of no bearing on the present argument) is the creature of the same degraded suffrage as returns a member of Parliament; he is chosen by the same ignorant, unscrupulous, gullible, bribable voters; he is presumably exposed to the same low motives that, according to Mr. Lecky, everybody knows to be acquiring greater and greater prominence in English politics. Yet the town-councillor is enthroned on high for our admiration, a worthy rival in public spirit of ancient Greece, mediæval Italy, Flanders, and the free towns of the Baltic, while the same electors who choose such a being for local purposes, no sooner think of purposes imperial, than 'the highest self-governing qualities' vanish from their minds, and we have as the final result the wretched and unholy spectacle which Mr. Lecky now watches in melancholy mood every day at Westminster—much like the hapless country maiden whom, in the first of his pictures of a certain unfortunate female's progress, Hogarth represents alighting from the coach in wicked London, to find herself in the midst of a scandalous troop of panders and procuresses.

In passing, I should like with all humility to say a word for the House of Commons, of whose character Mr. Lecky thinks so meanly, whose power he is so anxious to fetter, and in whose permanence as a governing institution he has so little faith. He writes as if the House were all rhetoric and tactics and bear-garden. It is nothing of the sort. 'No one,' he says, can be insensible to the change in the tone of the House of Commons within the memory of living men,' and he means change for the worse. Now the tone of an assembly is just one of the things about which a wise man will be slow to dogmatise, unless he has had a long opportunity of frequenting the assembly, feeling its atmosphere, and living its life. Tone is a subtle thing. You may judge a speech, or an Act of Parliament, or a piece of policy, at your own fireside, but you will never from that distance know enough of the tone of a legislature to warrant very confident assertions about it; and Mr. Lecky, as he says, and as we are all to our great advantage aware, has been for years 'deeply immersed' in the affairs of the eighteenth century. In truth this is a question on which the oldest parliamentary hands will perhaps think twice and thrice before saying either 'Aye' or 'No.' Men will judge for themselves. For my own part, after five-and-twenty years of experience, my strong impression is that in all the elements that go to compose what we may take Mr. Lecky to mean by tone—respect for sincerity, free tolerance of unpopular opinion, manly considerateness, quick and sure response to high appeal in public duty and moral feeling, a strong spirit of fair-play (now at last extended *bon gré, mal gré* even to members from Ireland)—that in these and the like things, the House of Commons has not deteriorated, but on the contrary has markedly improved. Moral elements have come forward into greater consideration, they have not fallen back into less.[1]

It is well to remember that, though the House of Commons is a council met to deliberate, the deliberation is for the most part by way of contention and conflict. This may or may not be the best way of getting the national business done, and of course it is accompanied all day long by a vast abundance of underlying co-operation. But con-

[1] The House of Commons chosen in 1906 contains a good many exponents of ideas that I do not happen to share, but in manners, and in the virtues above enumerated, it is the best of the seven parliaments in which I have sat.

tention is what engages most interest, kindles most energy, brings into play most force, is the centre of most effort. It may not be the most beautiful spectacle in the world—ceaseless contention never can be; it is not always favourable to the Christian graces; there is more serenity in a library, though, for that matter, books and bookmen have been ablaze with furious contention before now; there is more stillness in a cloister, though all is not sanctity, all is not exemption from strife and rivalry, even in a cloister. In the arena where material interests are touched, where deep political passions are stirred, where coveted prizes are lost and won, where power and the fleeting breath of a day's fame are at stake, where, under the rules and semblance of a tournament, men are fighting what is in truth a keen and not an ignoble battle, it is really childish to apply the tests of scholastic fastidiousness. We have to take the process as it is, and I very confidently submit that it is now conducted, not with less right feeling, considerateness, elevation, talent, knowledge, and respect for talent and knowledge, than was the case in the memory of living men, as Mr. Lecky says, but with very much more of all these things.

It is only natural that, where the main theory of the book shows so violent a bias, the same heated partiality should mark treatment of detail. I have only space for one or two out of a multitude of illustrations.

The power of arbitrarily closing debates, Mr. Lecky says, has been grossly abused. The only instance that occurs to him is the Home Rule Bill of 1893. Many clauses of that measure, he tells us, going, as they did, to the root of the constitution, were passed without the smallest possibility of discussion. It has altogether escaped his impartial memory that the very same treatment he thinks so shameless in 1893, six years earlier befell another measure that also went to the roots of the constitution, for it empowered the executive government in Ireland, at its own will and pleasure, to deprive of trial by jury prisoners charged with offences in which the protection of a jury is in England held to be most vital; and this power, moreover, was left in the hands of the government in perpetuity. So, too, it has slipped from his recollection that precisely in the same fashion, or worse, was passed the Act creating the Parnell Commission, perhaps the most unconstitutional measure of its century, by which certain men were brought before a special tribunal, constituted absolutely at the discretion of their bitterest political opponents, and with the scope and limit of the inquiry determined by those opponents against the remonstrance and protest of the persons most deeply concerned. If the closure of 1893 was a gross abuse, what was the closure of 1887, and the closure of 1888?

Here, again, is a case, not of failure of memory, but of perversion of fact:

The gigantic corruption which exists in America under the name of the spoils system has not taken root in England, though *some recent attempts to tamper in the interests of party* with the old method of appointing magistrates in the counties . . . show that there are politicians who would gladly introduce this poison-germ into English life (i. 129).

But is this particular poison-germ so recent, and has tampering with the appointment of magistrates in the interests of party never been heard of before? Let us look first at Mr. Lecky's own country. In that country, broadly speaking, and for the purposes of this argument, religious distinctions coincide with party distinctions. The late Liberal government appointed 637 county justices over the heads of the lieutenants of counties. Of these, 554 were Roman Catholics and 83 were Protestants. But let us see how the balance of the two religious communions stands even after this operation. The total number of justices on the benches of Irish counties up to July 1895 was 5412. Of this total, the Roman Catholics numbered in all no more than 1720, out of whom (including those added with the assent of lieutenants of counties) the Liberal government was responsible for about 750. That is to say, finding that the old system had planted some 3700 magistrates of one party on the county benches, as against less than 1000 of the other, we made a singularly moderate effort to bring the balance a trifle nearer to justice and reason, by reducing the old ascendancy from being between three and four to one, to the proportion of rather more than two to one. And this is the step which, in a country where, firstly, the majority of two to one on the bench is a minority of one to three in the population, and where, secondly, the petty sessions court is the place where the administration of law and justice comes closest home to the daily life of the people—this is the step which our high philosophic censor describes as tampering with sacred usage in the interests of party, and introducing the poison-germ of the spoils system into our public life. Detachment of mind is a very fine thing, but a serious writer should not wholly detach himself from the reality of the matter he happens to be writing about.

In Lancashire, the Chancellor of the Duchy exposed himself to Mr. Lecky's benign innuendo by endeavouring to diminish the disparity between the two parties. How had the old method, which Mr. Lecky so admires, and which his party have now restored, actually worked? From 1871 to 1886 the percentage of Liberals to Tories in the appointments to the county bench was about 45 to 55. From 1886 to 1893 the percentage of Liberals was only 20, against 80 per cent belonging to the opposite party or parties. Here, too, the poison-germ was older than Mr. Lecky thought. As regards England generally, Mr. Lecky ought to be glad to know that the Lord Chancellor, in 1892, found on almost every borough bench a great majority of Tory magistrates, even in places where Liberals were largely preponderant; yet in no single borough did he by his additions put his own party in a majority, nor in most cases did he even put it on an equality. As for the counties, the Chancellor left the Tories everywhere in a majority, and the total number of appointments of those who were not recommended by the lord-lieutenant of the county was extremely small. The 'new Jesuits' may really, like Lord Clive, stand aghast at their own moderation, and Mr. Lecky may stand aghast at his own gifts of heedless misrepresentation.

One of the strangest of his many stumbles is to be found in his story of the Indian cotton duties (i. 207). To illustrate the danger to India of our system of feeble governments, disintegrated Parliaments, and ignorant constituencies, he mentions 'the policy which forbade India in a time of deep financial distress to raise a revenue by import duties on English cotton, in accordance with the almost unanimous desire of her administrators and her educated public opinion.' An agitation was raised in England, and 'both parties' feared to run the electoral risk. But is this true ? Have both parties feared to run the risk ? Mr. Lecky in the next sentence shows that his own statement is untrue, and that one party did not by any means fear to run the risk. For he goes on to say that the Indian Secretary of the day had the courage to insist on revising the false step, 'and he found sufficient patriotism in the Opposition to enable him to secure the support of a large majority in the House of

Commons.' But the Indian Secretary was the member of a weak Government (and Mr. Lecky can hardly suppose that he took such a step as this without the assent of his colleagues, risk or no risk); he represents a popular, and therefore, according to Mr. Lecky, an ignorant, constituency; and he appealed successfully to a disintegrated Parliament. A more maladroit illustration of our woeful plight could not be found.

As for the patriotism of the Opposition, it is worth remembering that the gentleman who is now Indian Secretary, and who then spoke from the front Opposition bench, stoutly resisted the view that Mr. Lecky so rightly applauds, and he vouched in support of his resistance Lord Salisbury himself,[1] the head of the party—who does not sit for an ignorant constituency, but is Chancellor of the University of Oxford, and may therefore presumably be taken for a grand quintessential sublimation of the political wisdom and virtue of those Masters of Arts to whom Mr. Lecky looks for the salvation of our national affairs. Such a presentation of fact and of argument is really below the level of the flimsiest campaign leaflet.

Not seldom is the sin of inaccuracy added to the sin of gross partisanship. The author thinks, for example, that the abolition of the London coal and wine dues was a mistake. But he does not stop there. 'Not one Londoner in a hundred,' he argues, 'even knew of the existence of the small duty on

[1] *Hansard*, February 21, 1895, p. 1354.

coal which was abolished by the London County Council.' The London County Council could no more have abolished the coal dues, than it could disestablish the Church. That step was taken by Parliament, under the guidance of a Tory Chancellor of the Exchequer, and with the full approval of those experienced official advisers to whom Mr. Lecky looks as the mainstay of decent administration. The new voters, after all, are not the only ignorant people who presume to meddle with politics.

In another place he remarks that, ' chiefly through the influence of the Socialist members of the County Council, that body has . . . brought back the system of " make-wages," or " rates in aid of wages," which had long been regarded by economists as one of the worst abuses of the earlier years of the century.' It has done this by ' fixing a minimum rate of wages, irrespective of the value of the work performed, and considerably higher than that for which equally efficient labour could be easily obtained.'

A more exaggerated, confused, and misleading statement could hardly be made. That the Council should make some mistakes at first was natural; but they soon repaired them, and at any time to talk of their bringing back rates in aid of wages is pure moonshine. The standing order requires that in works done by the Council without the intervention of a contractor the wages and hours ' shall be based on the rates of wages and hours of labour recognised, and in practice obtained, by the various trade unions in London.' Any contractor, in like manner, employed by the Council shall bind himself to conform to these same conditions as to wages and hours. The London School Board imposes the same conditions. The House of Commons has, by unanimous resolution, directed the government to make every effort to secure the payment of such wages as are generally accepted as current in each trade for competent workmen. Is all this, either in principle or practice, more than Mr. Lecky does for himself when he engages a servant ? He pays the servant, not the very lowest sum that would enable such a servant to keep body and soul together, but a sum regulated partly by custom, partly by competition, partly by his own idea of what is reasonable, kind, and decent. If Mr. Lecky had only taken the trouble to cross the floor of the House, Mr. John Burns or Mr. Buxton would have told him the whole story in a quarter of an hour, and saved him from making himself an illustration of the great truth, that nothing makes men reason so badly as ignorance of the facts.

The statement that the House of Commons 'had been, after the Revolution of 1688, the most powerful element of the Constitution,' is surely a mistake. Speaker Onslow used to declare that the Septennial Bill of 1716 marked the true era of the emancipation of the House of Commons from its former dependence on the Crown and the House of Lords. Nor did its emancipation at once raise it to be the most powerful element of the Constitution; among other reasons, because powerful members of the House of Lords were the grand electors of a majority in the House of Commons. In fact, Mr. Lecky corrects his own error when he says (i. 310) that it was the Reform Bill of 1832 which fundamentally altered the position of the House of Lords in the constitution, deprived it of its claim to be a co-ordinate power with the House of Commons, and thrust it definitely into a secondary position.

It is incorrect to say (ii. 125) that licensing justices act under the supervision and control of the central government. The central government has no part in the business. If by central government Mr. Lecky means the courts of law—rather an unusual construction—the magistrates are only under their supervision and control, in exactly the same sense in which any of us exercise our discretion in anything; that is to say, if magistrates break the law in licensing or any other business, they may be brought into court. To tell us this is to tell us nothing, and what Mr. Lecky says is misleading and incorrect.

One small error in contemporary history, it is perhaps worth while to set right. 'It is notorious that the most momentous new departure made by the Liberal party in our day—the adoption of the policy of Home Rule—was due to a single man, who acted without consultation with his colleagues' (i. 24). Whatever may be said of the first part of this sentence, Mr. Lecky must have been aware that the allegation that the single man acted without consultation with his former colleagues rests on mere gossip, and he must know that gossip of this sort is the most untrustworthy thing in the world. As it happens, the gossip is untrue.

The most rapid examination of the bitter prejudice and partisanship of the present work must include the episode of Irish land. The author's great case in illustration of the tendency in a democratic system to what he calls class bribery, is the legislation of the last six-and-twenty years affecting Irish land. To this still burning theme he devotes, as I have already said, nearly forty pages, and pages less adequate, less impartial, looser as history, weaker as political philosophy, and blinder as regards political practice, it has not been my fortune, after a fairly wide acquaintance with this exhilarating department of literature, ever before to come across.

First, as to the history of the relations between the owners and the occupiers of land. There were 'grave faults on both sides,' says Mr. Lecky affably: 'wretched farming; thriftless, extravagant, unbusinesslike habits in all classes; a great want of enterprise and steady industry; much neglect of duty, and occasional, though not, I think, frequent, acts of extortion' (i. 139). The ordinary ignorant English reader will suppose from these smooth phrases that 'all classes' stood on something like equal terms, social, political, moral, economic. The Irish landlord and the Irish cottier, before and for many years after the Famine, hardly stood on more equal terms than did the Carolina planter and his negro.

The Irish tenant, whose status was a desperate status, and who clung with the tenacity of a drowning man to his cabin and patch of potato-ground—what is the sense of talking of his wretched farming, his thriftlessness and extravagance, as if it were in some way on a par with the extravagance and thriftlessness of Castle Rackrent ? And as for the wretched farming, who could wonder that the farming was wretched, when every attempt at improvement exposed the improver to a rise of rent as a consequence of it ? Bentham said a hundred years ago that the Turkish government had in his time impoverished some of the richest countries in the world, far more by its influence on motives than by its positive exactions. This is the explanation of the backward slovenly habits which Mr. Lecky sets down as a sort of counterweight to the oppression, extortion, and neglect of duty that were in truth their cause. Nobody knows better than Mr. Lecky the real root of the situation making land legislation of some sort an absolute necessity. It has been described a score of times, from the days of Arthur Young downwards, but by nobody more convincingly than by Sir G. Cornewall Lewis in that admirable book on the cause of Irish disturbances, which, in spite of its inadequate positive suggestions, one could wish that every public man, or every private man for that matter, who thinks about Ireland, would take the moderate pains to master. Anybody can now see that a revolution was sooner or later inevitable, as it was, whether later or sooner, thoroughly justifiable. Even before the Famine, Mr. Disraeli, in famous sentences, declared that it was the business of statesmen to effect by policy what revolution would effect by force.

Yet from one single point of view only, and from no other whatever, does Mr. Lecky allow himself or us to regard this striking, complex, and dangerous situation. It is intolerable to him that the statesman should introduce a single ingredient into his remedial plan, that cannot be obviously reconciled with the strictest and narrowest interpretation of the legal rights of property. He does not deny that there were cases where the raising of the rents led to 'a virtual confiscation of tenants' improvements' (i. 139); and a more impartial historian would find abundant evidence for putting it vastly higher than this. Yet he speaks with truly edifying indignation of the League appeals to the cupidity of the Irish electors. That is to say, what in the landlord is a noble stand for the rights of property, is criminal cupidity in the tenant who resents the confiscation of his improvements. 'To me, at least,' Mr. Lecky says in a singularly innocent passage, 'the first and greatest service a Government can render to morals seems to be the maintenance of a social organisation in which the path of duty and the path of interest as much as possible coincide ; in which honesty, industry, providence, and public spirit naturally reap their

rewards, and the opposite vices their punishment'
(i. 169).

This is impressive enough, and nobody will dissent from it. It is exactly what the Irish tenant said. This is the very service which, first in 1870 and then in 1881, Irish agitation compelled the British government to 'render to morals.' How else could the honesty, industry, and providence of the tenant be rewarded, and the greed, idleness, and extravagance of his landlord receive its punishment, except by laws protecting the tenant in property which his own labour had created? The agrarian revolutionists were, on Mr. Lecky's own principle, the true moralists and evangelists, and the shame rests on the statesmen and the Parliaments that made revolutionary action inevitable. It was the Land League that drove the government to protect industry and providence by the legislation of 1881, and when Mr. Lecky talks in the ordinary vein of intimidation, greed, political agitators and the rest of it, he forgets the memorable answer of Sir Redvers Buller before the Cowper Commission. He was asked whether there was any general sympathy with the action of the League on the part of the people. 'Yes,' he answered, ' I think there is sympathy, because they think that it has been their salvation. . . . *Nobody did anything for the tenants until the League was established.*' [1] This is an old story, but it will have to be told over and over again, so long as writers of

[1] Question 16494. November 11, 1886.

authority, like Mr. Lecky, abuse the credulous ignorance of English readers.

Even the famous Act for the compulsory sale of encumbered estates is too much for Mr. Lecky. And, by the way, we wonder why he talks of that measure as having been put forward by the Whig party as the supreme remedy for the ills of Ireland. He must know Irish history far too well to be ignorant that Peel was much more truly its author than Russell, and that without Peel's energetic support it would not have been carried. But let this little perversion of history pass. He quotes (i. 151), apparently with agreement, a long extract from an eminent lawyer, describing the cruel injustice with which, under this Act, some of the most ancient and respected families in the country, whose estates were not encumbered to much more than half their value, were sold out and beggared by the harshness of the Liberal party. Let me quote a few lines from a writer whose authority and judicial temper Mr. Lecky will not be slow to admit. Speaking of the encumbered landlords dealt with under the Act, the late J. E. Cairnes wrote :

It would be a mistake to regard these men—albeit their final overthrow happened to be accomplished by the famine and the measures which that event rendered necessary—as the victims of this particular crisis in Irish history. Like the ruin of the Jamaica planters, which, though consummated by the Emancipation Act and free trade, had through half a century been steadily maturing under the pre-existing state of things—a state of things not very dissimilar from that which had prevailed in

Ireland—the fate of this class of Irish squires had been sealed long before the famine, free trade, or the Encumbered Estates Court had been heard of. In the case of a large majority, their indebtedness dated from an early period of the century, and was, in fact, the direct result of their own reckless and extravagant habits—habits, no doubt, quite naturally engendered by their situation. . . . The famine and the measures which it necessitated can only be regarded as precipitating an inevitable catastrophe, and the Act merely gave the sanction of law to what were already accomplished facts.[1]

Of course, in any work pretending to be of value in political philosophy or political history, the view of Cairnes would have been given along with the views of Fitzgibbon and Butt, that the reader might at least have a chance of knowing that there were two sides to the question. But Mr. Lecky is thinking of things a long way removed from political philosophy.

We must follow him a little further. He says that the tenants preferred making their improvements in their own economical, and generally slovenly, way, rather than have them made in the English fashion by the landlord. This is wholly misleading. The Irish landlord did not make the improvements because his tenants preferred their own slovenly ways, but for the very simple reason that he could not make them. The holdings on an estate were so small, and therefore so numerous, that nobody but a

[1] *Political Essays.* By J. E. Cairnes. Published in 1873, but this fragment was written in 1866.

millionaire could possibly have equipped each of
them with buildings, fences, drains, as an English
farm is equipped. This is the well-understood
explanation of the difference between the Irish and
the English systems. Nobody blames the landlord
for not making the improvements. What he is
blamed for is the extortion of rent for the improvements which the tenant made for himself.

Hence the absurdity of the statement that among
other effects of the legislation of 1881, it has withdrawn
the whole rental of Ireland from the improvement of
the soil, ' as the landlord can have no further inducement or obligation to spend money on his estate '
(i. 167). With rare exceptions it is notorious, and
the Select Committee of 1894 only brought it into
clearer light, that the landlord scarcely ever felt this
inducement and obligation, any more than he feels
it now.

Not any less absurd are the other items in the
catalogue of disasters alleged to be due to the legislation of 1881. ' In a poor country, where increased
capital, improved credit, and secure industry are
the greatest needs, it has shaken to the very basis
the idea of the sanctity and obligation of contract;
made it almost impossible to borrow any considerable
sum on Irish land; effectually stopped the influx
of English gold; has reacted powerfully upon trade,'
and so forth (i. 167). There is the familiar accent
of the *émigré* in every line of this. *Ils prennent leurs
souvenirs pour des droits*, and then because they

have had their claws clipped, they vow that the country is ruined. 'Secure industry' is indeed, as the author truly says, one of the greatest of Irish needs ; but security in the one great industry of the island is exactly what the Act of 1881 aimed at, and in a very considerable degree, in spite of defects brought to light by experience, has actually achieved. As for the terrible reaction upon trade, Mr. Lecky must live with his eyes shut to the most patent facts in the state of commercial Ireland for the last three or four years. Never have Irish railways and banks been so prosperous as they are to-day, after this Act has been for fifteen years impoverishing and demoralising the country. As for 'driving much capital out of the land,' one would like to have some definite evidence of the extent of any such process. And as for the impossibility of borrowing any considerable sum on Irish land, one would like to know first whether the owner can borrow any considerable sum on a great deal of English land ; second, whether the considerable sums that were borrowed in times past on Irish land ever did any good either to the landowner or to anybody else, or whether the old facility of borrowing money to be squandered in riotous and swaggering folly, has not been the worst of all the many curses of Ireland.

To probe these forty pages on Irish land would need as many pages more. So let us pass on. The rigour and inelasticity of Mr. Lecky's conception of the institution of Property prevent his chapter on

Socialism from being a contribution of any real importance to that subject. His commonplace books supply an account of the more influential Socialist writers, but he submits them to no searching criticism, and he plants himself on ground that deprives him of real influence over anybody's mind upon the controversy. He talks, for instance (ii. 304), of the sense of right and wrong being the basis of respect for property and for the obligation of contract. This will never do. It begs the whole question. The Socialist believes that he can make an unanswerable case the other way, namely for the proposition that the unsophisticated sense of right and wrong, so far from being the root of respect for property, is hostile to it, and is at this moment shaking it to its foundation all over the modern world. After the parliamentary reform of 1867, Mill with his usual patient sagacity foresaw, and began a series of systematic speculations upon the strength of foreseeing, that as the new electorate are not engaged by any peculiar interest of their own to the support of property as it is, least of all to the support of the inequalities of property, therefore henceforth, wherever the power of the new electorate reaches, the laws of property will no longer be able to depend upon motives of a mere personal character, operating on the minds of those who have control over the government. The classes, he observed, which the present system of society makes subordinate, have little reason to put faith in any of the maxims the same system of society may have established as principles. All plans for attaining the benefits aimed at by the institution of property without its inconveniences, should be examined with candour, and not prejudged as absurd or impracticable.[1] Mr. Lecky does little more than what the writer of those few pages of such calm gravity particularly warned us not to do. He only confronts prejudice with prejudice, and leaves the battle to be fought out between 'ignorant change and ignorant opposition to change.'

Socialism brings us to Militarism. Undoubtedly one of the most remarkable of all the circumstances of the democratic dispensation, however we put it, is its failure as a guarantee of international peace. Mr. Lecky says that there is a growing feeling in the most civilised portions of Europe in favour of universal military service (i. 256). Some publicists here and there may have vamped up afresh the plausible sophisms glorifying the noble effects upon character of the drill-ground, the barrack, the battlefield, but the signs are few that nations follow them, or agree with them. And Mr. Lecky himself has noted the decisive evidence against his own statement. After an elaborate exposition of the case for the barrack, he winds up, one is glad to think for his own credit, though in rather halting sentences, with the judgment that though the panegyrists of the blessings of universal military service have undoubtedly something

[1] *Fortnightly Review*, February, March, April, 1879. 'Chapters on Socialism.'

to say for themselves, yet on the whole more is to be said against them. The military system, he thinks, may do much to employ and reclaim 'the dangerous classes'—spectres ever present to his alarmed mind—but still it has the unlucky incidental drawback of bringing burdens that are steadily fomenting discontent. That is to say, this handy device for employing and reclaiming the dangerous classes, unfortunately at the same moment and by the same process, breeds new dangerous classes, extends the area of their operations, and profoundly intensifies the irritation and discontent that makes the danger. 'Certainly,' says Mr. Lecky, 'the great military nations of the world are not those in which Anarchy, Socialism, and Nihilism are least rife.' Quite true; and the extraordinarily rapid growth of revolutionary Socialism in continental Europe, of which the author gives so full an account (ii. ch. 8), and which is one of the two or three most important phenomena of our time, is the direct and unmistakable result of militarism, and the vehement protest against it.

Nothing in political meditation can be more deeply interesting, than the connection between universal military service and universal suffrage. Taine says that each of them is twin brother of the other. Every citizen, said the early Jacobins, ought to be a soldier, every soldier a citizen. We can understand why the Jacobin, with the Duke of Brunswick and the coalition of kings on the frontier, said this. But what is the secret of the operation that places a ballot paper in one hand of every citizen, and at the same instant a rifle in the other? 'With what promises of massacre and bankruptcy for the twentieth century, with what exasperation of hatred and distrust between nations, with what destruction and waste of human toil and the fruits of it . . . with what a recoil towards the lower and unwholesome forms of the old militant societies, with how retrograde a step towards the egotistic and brutal instincts, the sentiments, the manners, the morality of the ancient city and of barbarous tribes.'[1]

No other effect of democracy is comparable with this, no other so surprising, no other so widely at variance with confident and reasoned anticipations. We can only be sure that a retrograde military and diplomatic phase must be due to deeper influences than those belonging to democracy as a mere form of government, and must have its roots in the hidden and complex working of those religious and scientific ideas which at all times have exercised a preponderating influence upon human institutions and their working.

Such questions are left almost unexplored by Mr. Lecky. Nor can he be said to have advanced any other portion of his subject beyond the position in which he found it. That democracy has drawbacks,

[1] *Origines de la France contemporaine: régime moderne*, i. 288.

that it has difficulties of its own and weaknesses and dangers of its own, both in this country and elsewhere, every observant man is well aware. They assuredly deserve to be considered in a different spirit from that which marks these volumes.

MAINE ON POPULAR GOVERNMENT.[1]

'IF the government of the Many,' says the distinguished author of the volume before us, ' be really inevitable, one would have thought that the possibility of discovering some other and newer means of enabling it to fulfil the ends for which all governments exist, would have been a question exercising all the highest powers of the strongest minds, particularly in the community which, through the success of its popular institutions, has paved the way for modern Democracy. Yet hardly anything worth mentioning has been produced on the subject in England or on the Continent.' To say this, by the way, is strangely to ignore three or four very remarkable books that have been published within the last twenty or five-and-twenty years, that have excited immense attention and discussion, and are the work of minds Sir Henry Maine would hardly call weak or inactive. We are no adherents of any of Mr. Hare's proposals, but there are important public men who think that his work on the Election of Representatives is as conspicuous a landmark in politics as the *Principia*

[1] February 1886.

was in natural philosophy. J. S. Mill's *Considerations on Representative Government*, which appeared in 1861, was even a more memorable contribution towards the solution of the very problem defined by Sir Henry Maine, than was the older Mill's article on Government in 1820 to the political difficulties of the eve of the Reform Bill. Again, Lord Grey's work on Parliamentary Government failed in making its expected mark on legislation, but it was worth mentioning because it goes on the lines of the very electoral law in Belgium which Sir Henry Maine (p. 109) describes as deserving our respectful attention, which it is as little likely to receive. Nor should we neglect Sir G. C. Lewis's little book, or Mr. Harrison's volume, *Order and Progress*, which abounds in important criticism and suggestion for the student of the abstract politics of modern societies. In the United States, too, and in our own colonies, there have been attempts, not without merit, to state and to deal with some of the drawbacks of popular government.

Nothing has been done, however, that makes the appearance in the field of a mind of so high an order as Sir Henry Maine's either superfluous or unwelcome. It is hardly possible that he should discuss any subject within the publicist's range, without bringing into light some of its less superficial aspects, and adding observations of originality and value to the stock of political thought. To set people thinking at all on the more general and abstract truths of the great subject that is commonly left to be handled lightly, unsystematically, fragmentarily, in obedience to the transitory necessities of the day, by ministers, members of Parliament, journalists, electors, and the whole host who live intellectually and politically from hand to mouth, is in itself a service of all but the first order. Service of the very first order is not merely to propound objections, but to devise working answers, and this is exactly what Sir Henry Maine abstains from doing.

No one will think the moment for a serious political inquiry ill chosen. We have just effected an immense recasting of our system of parliamentary representation. The whole consequences of the two great Acts of 1884 and 1885 are assuredly not to be finally gauged by anything that has happened during the recent election. Yet even this single election has brought about a crisis of vast importance in one part of the United Kingdom, by forcing the question of an Irish constitution to the front. It is pretty clear, also, that the infusion of a large popular element into the elective House has made more difficult the maintenance of its old relations with the hereditary House. Even if there were no others, these two questions alone, and especially the first of them, will make the severest demands on the best minds in the country. We shall be very fortunate if the crisis produces statesmen as sagacious as those American publicists of whom Sir Henry Maine rightly entertains so exalted an opinion.

Whether or not we are on the threshold of great

legislative changes, it is in any case certain that the work of government will be carried on under new parliamentary and social conditions. In meeting this prospect, we have the aid neither of strong and systematic political schools, nor powerful and coherent political parties. No one can pretend, for instance, that there is any body of theoretic opinion so compact and so well thought out as Benthamism was in its own day and generation. Again, in practice, there are ominous signs that Parliament is likely to break up into groups ; and the substitution of groups for parties is certain, if continental experience is to count for anything, to create new obstacles in the way of firm and stable government. Weak government throws power to something that usurps the name of public opinion, and public opinion, as expressed by the ventriloquists of the newspapers, is at once more capricious and more vociferous than it ever was. This was abundantly shown during the last five years by a variety of unfortunate public adventures. Then, does the excitement of democracy weaken the stability of national temperament ? By setting up what in physics would be called a highly increased molecular activity, does it disturb not merely conservative respect for institutions, but respect for coherence and continuity of opinion and sentiment in the character of the individual himself ? Is there a fluidity of character in modern democratic societies that contrasts not altogether favourably with the strong solid types of old ? These and many other considerations of the same kind are enough to secure a ready welcome for any thinker who can light up the obscurities of the time.

With profound respect, as we need not say, for Sir Henry Maine's attainments, and every desire to profit by illumination wherever it may be discerned, we cannot clearly see how the present volume either makes the problems more intelligible, or points the way to feasible solutions. Though he tries, in perfect good faith, to be the dispassionate student, he often comes very close to the polemics of the hour. The truth is that scientific lawyers have seldom been very favourable to popular government, and when the scientific lawyer is doubled with the Indian bureaucrat, we are pretty sure beforehand that in such a tribunal it will go hard with democracy. That the author extremely dislikes and suspects the new order, he does not hide either from himself or us. Intellectual contempt for the idolatries of the forum and the market-place has infected him with a touch of the chagrin that came to men like Tacitus from disbelief in the moral government of a degenerate world. Though he strives, like Tacitus, to take up his parable *nec amore et sine odio*, the disgust is ill concealed. There are passages where we almost hear the drone of a dowager in the Faubourg Saint-Germain. It was said of Tocqueville that he was an aristocrat who accepted his defeat. Sir Henry Maine in politics is a bureaucrat who cannot bear to think that democracy will win. He is dangerously near the frame of mind of Scipio Emilianus, after the movement of the Gracchi and the opening of the Roman revolution. Scipio came to the conclusion that with whichever party he took sides, or whatever measures a disinterested and capable statesman might devise, he would only aggravate the evil. Sir Henry Maine would seem to be nearly as despondent. Hence his book is fuller of apprehension than of guidance, more plausible in alarm than wise or useful in direction. It is exclusively critical and negative. There is, indeed, an admirable account of the constitution of the United States. But on the one great question on which the constitution of the United States might have been expected to shed light—the modification of the House of Lords—Sir Henry Maine explicitly admits (p. 186) that it is very difficult to obtain from the younger institution, the Senate, any lessons that can be of use in the reconstruction of the older. At every turn, the end of the discussion lands us in a philosophical *cul-de-sac*, and nothing is so depressing as a *cul-de-sac*. The tone is that of the political valetudinarian, watching with uneasy eye the ways of rude health. Unreflecting optimism about Popular Government is sickening, but calculated pessimism is not much better.

Something, no doubt, may often be gained by the mere cross-examination of catchwords and the exposure of platitudes. Popular government is no more free from catchwords and platitudes than any other political, religious, or social cause that interests a great many people, and is the subject of much discussion. Even the Historical Method has its own clap-trap. But one must not make too much of these things. 'In order to love mankind,' said Helvétius, 'one must not expect too much from them.' And fairly to appreciate institutions you must not hold them up against the light that blazes in Utopia; you must not expect them to satisfy microscopic analysis, nor judge their working, which is inevitably rough, awkward, clumsy, and second-best, by the fastidious standards of closet logic.

Before saying more as to the substance of the book, we may be allowed to notice one or two matters of literary or historical interest in which Sir Henry Maine is certainly open to criticism. There is an old question about Burke that was discussed by the present writer a long time ago. A great disillusion, says Sir Henry Maine, has always seemed to him to separate the *Thoughts on the Present Discontents* and the *Speech on Taxation* from the magnificent panegyric on the British Constitution in 1790. 'Not many persons in the last century could have divined from the previous opinions of Edmund Burke the real sub-structure of his political creed, or did in fact suspect it till it was uncovered by the early and comparatively slight miscarriage of French revolutionary institutions.' This is, as a statement of fact, not at all correct. Lord Chatham detected what he believed to be the mischievous Conservatism in Burke's constitutional doctrines at the very outset. So did the Constitutional Society detect it. So did Mrs.

Macaulay, Bishop Watson, and many other people. The story of Burke's inconsistency is, of course, as old as Sheridan. Hazlitt declared that the Burke of 1770 and the Burke of 1790 were not merely opposite persons, but deadly enemies. Buckle, who is full of veneration for the early writings, but dislikes the later ones, gets over the difficulty by insisting that Burke actually went out of his mind after 1789. We should have expected a subtler judgment from Sir Henry Maine. Burke belonged from first to last to the great historic and positive school, of which the founder was Montesquieu. Its whole method, principle, and sentiment, all animated him with equal force, whether he was defending the secular pomps of Oude, the sanctity of Benares, the absolutism of Versailles, or the free and ancient Parliament at Westminster.[1]

Versailles reminds us of a singular overstatement by Sir Henry Maine of the blindness of the privileged classes in France to the approach of the Revolution. He speaks as if Lord Chesterfield's famous passage were the only anticipation of the coming danger. There is at least one utterance of Louis XV. himself, which shows that he did not expect things to last much beyond his time. D'Argenson, in the very year of Chesterfield's prophecy, pronounced that a revolution was inevitable, and he even went so close

---

[1] It is satisfactory to have the authority of Mr. Lecky on the same side. *England in the Eighteenth Century*, vol. iii. ch. ix. p. 209.

to the mark as to hint that it would arise on the first occasion when it should be necessary to convoke the States-General. Rousseau, in a page of the *Confessions*, not only divined a speedy revolution, but enumerated the operative causes of it with real precision. There is a striking prediction in Voltaire, and another in Mercier de la Rivière. Other names might be quoted to the same effect, including Maria Theresa, who described the ruined condition of the French monarchy, and only hoped that the ruin might not overtake her daughter. The mischief was not so much that the privileged classes were blind as that they were selfish, stubborn, helpless, and reckless. The point is not very important in itself, but it is characteristic of a very questionable way of reading human history. Sir Henry Maine's readiness to treat revolutions as due to erroneous abstract ideas naturally inclines him to take too narrow a view both of the preparation in circumstances, and of the preparation in the minds of observant onlookers.

In passing, by the way, we are curious to know the writer's authority for what he calls the odd circumstance that the Jacobins generally borrowed their phrases from the legendary history of the early Roman Republic, while the Girondins preferred to take metaphors from the literature of Rousseau (p. 75). There was plenty of nonsense talked about Brutus and Scævola by both parties, and it is not possible to draw the line with precision. But the received view is that the Girondins were Voltairean, and the Jacobins Rousseauite, while Danton was of the school of the Encyclopædia, and Hébert and Chaumette were inspired by Holbach.

The author seems to us greatly to exaggerate the whole position of Rousseau, and even in a certain sense to mistake the nature of his influence. That Jean Jacques was a far-reaching and important voice the present writer is not at all likely to deny; but no estimate of his influence in the world is correct that does not treat him rather as moralist than publicist. *Emilius* went deeper into men's minds in France and in Europe at large, and did more to quicken the democratic spirit, than the *Social Contract*. Apart from this, Sir Henry Maine places Rousseau on an isolated eminence that does not really belong to him. It did not fall within the limited scope of such an essay as Sir Henry Maine's to trace the leading ideas of the *Social Contract* to the various sources from which they had come, but his account of these sources is, even for its scale, inadequate. Portions of Rousseau's ideas, he says truly, may be discovered in the speculations of older writers; and he mentions Hobbes and the French Economists. But the most characteristic of all the elements in Rousseau's speculation were drawn from Locke. The theoretic basis of popular government is to be found in more or less definite shape in various authors from Thomas Aquinas downwards. But it was Locke's philosophic vindication of the Revolution of 1688, in the famous essay on Civil Government, that directly taught Rousseau the lesson of the Sovereignty of the People. Such originality as the *Social Contract* possesses is due to its remarkable union of the influence of the two antagonistic English Thinkers. The differences between Hobbes and Rousseau were striking enough. Rousseau looked on men as good, Hobbes looked on them as bad. The one described the state of nature as a state of peace, the other as a state of war. The first believed that laws and institutions had depraved man, the second that they had improved him. In spite of these differences the influence of Hobbes was important, but only important in combination. 'The total result is,' as I have said elsewhere, 'a curious fusion between the premisses and the temper of Hobbes, and the conclusions of Locke. This fusion produced that popular absolutism of which the *Social Contract* was the theoretical expression, and Jacobin supremacy the practical manifestation. Rousseau borrowed from Hobbes the true conception of sovereignty, and from Locke the true conception of the ultimate seat and original of authority, and of the two together he made the great image of the Sovereign People. Strike the crowned head from that monstrous figure which is the frontispiece of the *Leviathan*, and you have a frontispiece that will do excellently well for the *Social Contract*.'[1]

One more word may be said by the way. The very slightest account of Rousseau is too slight to be tolerable if it omits to mention Calvin. Rousseau's

[1] *Rousseau*, ii. 198.

whole theory of the Legislator, which produced such striking results in certain transitory phases of the French Revolution, grew up in his mind from the constitution which the great reformer had so predominant a share in framing for the little Republic where Rousseau was born. This omission of Locke and Calvin again exemplifies the author's characteristic tendency to look upon political ideas as if speculative writers got them out of their own heads, or out of the heads of other people, apart from the suggestions of events and the requirements of circumstance. Calvin was the builder of a working government, and Locke was the defender of a practical revolution.

Nor does the error stop at the literary sources of political theories. A point more or less in an estimate of a writer or a book is of trivial importance compared with what strikes us as Sir Henry Maine's tendency to impute an unreal influence to writers and books altogether. There is, no doubt, a vulgar and superficial opinion that mere speculation is so remote from the real interests of men, that it is a waste of time for practical people to concern themselves about speculation. No view could be more foolish, save one; and that one is the opposite view, that the real interests of men have no influence on their speculative opinions, and no share either in moulding those opinions, or in causing their adoption. Sir Henry Maine does not push things quite so far as this. Still he appears to us to attribute almost exclusive influence to political theories, and almost entirely to omit what we take to be the much more important reaction upon theory, both of human nature, and of the experience of human life and outward affairs. He makes no allowance among innovating agencies for native rationalism without a formula. His brilliant success in other applications of the Historic Method has disposed him to see survivals where other observers will be content with simpler explanations. The reader is sometimes tempted to recall Edie Ochiltree's rude interruption of Mr. Oldbuck's enthusiasm over the prætorium of the immortal Roman camp at Monkbarns. 'Prætorian here, prætorian there! I mind the bigging o't.'

Sir Henry Maine believes that the air is thick with ideas about democracy that were conceived *a priori*, and sprang from the teaching of Rousseau. A conviction of the advantages of legislative change, for example, he considers to owe its origin much less to active and original intelligence, than to 'the remote effect of words and notions derived from broken-down political theories' (p. 171). There are two great fountains of political theory in our country according to the author: Rousseau is one, and Bentham is the other. Current thought and speech is infested by the floating fragments of these two systems—by loose phrases, by vague notions, by superstitions, that enervate the human intellect and endanger social safety. This is the constant refrain of the pages before us. We should have liked better evidence. We do not believe that it is a Roman prætorium. Men often pick up old phrases for new events, even when they are judging events afresh with independent minds. When a politician of the day speaks of natural rights, he uses a loose traditional expression for a view of social equities that has come to him, not from a book, but from a survey of certain existing social facts. Now the phrase, the literary description, is the least significant part of the matter. When Mill talks of the influence of Bentham's writings, he is careful to tell us he does not mean that they caused the Reform Bill or the Appropriation Clause. 'The changes which have been made,' says Mill, 'and the greater changes which will be made, in our institutions are not the work of philosophers, but of the interests and instincts of large portions of society recently grown into strength' (*Dissertations*, i. 332). That is the point. It is the action of these interests and instincts that Sir Henry Maine habitually overlooks. Nor is the omission a mere speculative imperfection. It has an important bearing on the whole practical drift of the book. If he had made more room for 'the common intellect rough-hewing political truths at the suggestion of common wants and common experience,' he would have viewed existing circumstances with a less lively apprehension.

It is easy to find an apposite illustration of what is meant by saying that this talk of the influence of speculation is enormously exaggerated and misleading. When Arthur Young was in France in the autumn of 1787, he noticed a remarkable revolution in manners in two or three important respects. One of them was a new fashion that had just come in, of spending some weeks in the country: everybody who had a country seat went to live there, and such as had none went to visit those who had. This new custom, observed the admirable Young, is one of the best that they have taken from England, and 'its introduction was effected the easier being assisted by the magic of Rousseau's writings.' The other and more generally known change was that women of the first fashion were no longer ashamed of nursing their own children, and that infants were no longer tightly bound round by barbarous stays and swaddling clothes. This wholesome change, too, was assisted by Rousseau's eloquent pleas for simplicity and the life natural. Of these particular results of his teaching in France a hundred years ago the evidence is ample, direct, and beyond denial. But whenever we find gentlemen with a taste for country life, and ladies with a fancy for nursing their own children, we surely need not cry out that here is another proof of the extraordinary influence of the speculations of Jean Jacques Rousseau. We need not treat it as a survival of a broken-down theory. 'Great Nature is more wise than I,' says the Poet. Great Nature had much more to do with moulding men and women to these things than all the books that have ever been printed.

We are entirely sceptical as to the proposition that 'men have at all times quarrelled more fiercely about phrases and formulas than even about material interests' (p. 124). There has been a certain amount of fighting in the world about mere words, as idle as the faction fights between Caravats and Shanavests, or Two-Year-Olds and Three-Year-Olds in Ireland. But the more carefully we look into human history, the more apparent it becomes that underneath the phrase or the formula there is usually a material or a quasi-material, or a political, or a national, or an ecclesiastical interest. Few quarrels now seem so purely verbal as those that for several centuries raged about the mysteries of the faith in the Western and the Eastern Churches. Yet these quarrels, apparently as frivolous as they were ferocious, about the relations of mind and matter, about the composition of the Trinity, about the Divine nature, turned much less on futile metaphysics than on the solid competition for ecclesiastical power, or the conflict of rival nationalities. The most transcendental heresy or orthodoxy generally had what we call business at the bottom of it.

In limiting the parentage of modern English Liberalism of a radical or democratic type to Rousseau and Bentham, the author has left out of sight what is assuredly a much more important factor than any speculative, literary, or philosophic matter whatever. 'Englishmen,' he says truly, 'are wont to be content with the rough rule of success or failure as the test of right or wrong in national undertakings.' The same habit of mind and temper marks the attitude of Englishmen towards their national institutions. They look to success and failure, they take the measure of things from results, they consult the practical working of the machine, they will only go to school with experience. We cannot find the proof that *a priori* Radicalism ever at any time got a real hold of any considerable mass of the people of this country, or that any of the great innovations in domestic policy since the end of Lord Liverpool's administration have been inspired or guided by Rousseauite assumptions. Godwin, whose book on Political Justice was for a long time the great literary fountain of English Radicalism, owed quite as much to the utilitarian Helvétius as to the sentimental Rousseau. Nor can either William Cobbett or Joseph Hume be said to have dealt largely in *a priori*. What makes the Radical of the street, is mostly mother-wit exercising itself upon the facts of the time. His weakness is that he does not know enough of the facts of other times.

Sir Henry Maine himself points to what has had a far more decisive influence on English ways of thinking about politics than his two philosophers, put together. 'The American Republic,' he says (p. 11), 'has greatly influenced the favour into which popular government grew. It disproved the once universal assumptions that no Republic could govern a large territory, and that no strictly Republican government could be stable.' Nothing can be more true. When Burke and Chatham and Fox persistently declared that the victory of England over the colonists would prove fatal in the long run to the liberties of England itself, those great men were even wiser than they knew. The success of popular government across the Atlantic has been the strongest incentive to the extension of popular government here. We need go no further back than the Reform Bill of 1867 to remind ourselves that the victory of the North over the South, and the extraordinary clemency and good sense with which that victory was used, had more to do with the concession of the franchise to householders in boroughs than all the eloquence of Mr. Gladstone and all the diplomacies of Mr. Disraeli.

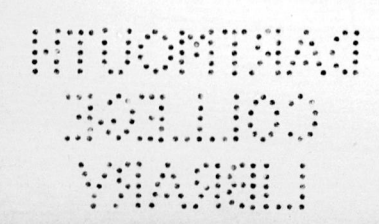

To the influence of the American Union must be added that of the British colonies. The success of popular self-government in these thriving communities is reacting on political opinion at home with a force that no statesman neglects, and that is every day increasing. There is even a danger that the influence may go too far. They are solving some of our problems, but not under our conditions, and not in presence of the same difficulties. Still the effect of colonial prosperity—a prosperity alike of admirable achievement and boundless promise—is irresistible. It imparts a freedom, an elasticity, an expansiveness, to English political notions, and gives our people a confidence in free institutions and popular government, that they would never have drawn from the most eloquent assumptions of speculative system-mongers, nor from any other source whatever, save practical experience carefully observed and rationally interpreted. This native and independent rationality in men is what the jealous votary of the historic method places far too low.

In coming closer to the main current of the book, our first disappointment is that Sir Henry Maine has not been very careful to do full justice to the views that he criticises. He is not altogether above lending himself to the hearsay of the partisan. He allows expressions to slip from him which show that he has not been anxious to face the problems of popular government as popular government is understood by those who have best right to speak for it. 'The more the difficulties of multitudinous government are probed,' he says (p. 180), 'the stronger grows the doubt of the infallibility of popularly elected legislatures.' We do not profess to answer for all that may have been said by Mr. Bancroft, or Walt Whitman, or all the orators of all the Fourths of July since American Independence. But we are not acquainted with any English writer or politician of the very slightest consideration or responsibility who has committed himself to the astounding proposition that popularly elected legislatures are infallible. Who has ever advanced such a doctrine? Further, 'It requires some attention to facts to see how widely spread is the misgiving as to the absolute wisdom of popularly elected chambers.' We are not surprised at the misgiving. But after reasonable attention to facts, we cannot recall any publicist whom it could be worth while to spend five minutes in refuting, who has ever said that popularly elected chambers are absolutely wise. Again, we should like the evidence for the statement that popularly elected Houses ' do not nowadays appeal to the wise deduction from experience, as old as Aristotle, which no student of constitutional history will deny, that the best constitutions are those in which there is a large popular element. It is a singular proof of the widespread influence of the speculations of Rousseau that although very few First Chambers really represent the entire community, nevertheless in Europe they almost invariably claim to reflect it, and as a consequence they assume an air of divinity, which if it rightfully belonged to them would be fatal to all argument for a Second Chamber.' That would be very important if it were true. But is it true that First Chambers assume an air of divinity? Or is such an expression a burlesque of the real argument? A reasonable familiarity with the course of the controversy in France, where the discussion has been abundant, and in England, where it has been comparatively meagre, leaves me, for one, entirely ignorant that this claim for divinity, or anything like it, is ever heard in the debate. The most powerful modern champion of popular government was Gambetta. Did Gambetta consider First Chambers divine? On the contrary, some of the most strenuous pleas for the necessity of a Second Chamber are to be found precisely in the speeches of Gambetta (*e.g.* his speech at Grenoble, in the autumn of 1878, *Discours*, viii. 270, etc.). Abstract thinking is thinking withdrawn from the concrete and particular facts. But the abstract thinker should not withdraw too far.

Sir Henry Maine speaks (p. 185) of ' the saner political theorist, who holds that in secular matters it is better to walk by sight than by faith.' He allows that a theorist of this kind, as regards popularly elected chambers, ' will be satisfied that experience has shown the best Constitutions to be those in which the popular element is large, and he will readily admit that, as the structure of each society of men slowly alters, it is well to alter and amend the organisation by which this element makes itself felt.' Sir Henry Maine would surely have done better service in this grave and difficult discussion, if he had dealt with views that he mistrusts, as they are really held and expressed by sane theorists, and not by insane theorists out of sight. In France, a hundred years ago, from causes that are capable of explanation, the democracy of sentiment swept away the democracy of utility. In spite of casual phrases in public discussion, and in spite of the incendiary trash of Red journalists without influence, it is the democracy of reason, experience, and utility that is now in the ascendant, both in France and elsewhere.

The same spirit of what we must call parody is shown in such a statement as that (p. 78) ' an audience composed of roughs or clowns is boldly told by an educated man that it has more political information

than an equal number of scholars.' By 'roughs'
Sir Henry Maine explains that he means the artisans
of the towns. The designation is hardly felicitous.
It is not even fashionable; for the roughs and clowns
are now, by common consent of Tories and Liberals
alike, transformed into capable citizens. Such a
phrase gives us a painful glimpse of the accurate
knowledge of their countrymen possessed by eminent
men who write about them from the dim and distant
seclusion of college libraries and official bureaux.
If Sir Henry Maine could spare a few evenings from
dispassionate meditations on popular government
in the abstract, to the inspection of the governing
people in the concrete, he would be the first to see
that to despatch an audience of skilled artisans as an
assembly of roughs is as unscientific, to use the mildest
word, as the habit in a certain religious world of
lumping all the unconverted races of the earth in
every clime and age in the summary phrase, the
heathen. A great meeting of artisans listening to
Mr. Arthur Balfour or Sir Henry Roscoe at Manchester,
to Sir Lyon Playfair at Leeds (the modern democrat,
at any rate, does not think the Republic has no need
of chemists), or to anybody else in a great industrial
centre anywhere else, is no more an assemblage of
roughs than Convocation or the House of Lords.
Decidedly, an enemy of the unverified assumptions
of democracy ought to be on his guard against the
unverified assumptions of pedantocracy.

As for the particular bit of sycophancy which

educated men wickedly dangle before roughs and clowns, we should like to be sure that the proposition is correctly reported. If the educated man tells his roughs (if that be the right name for the most skilful, industrious, and effective handicraftsmen in the world) that they have as much of the information necessary for shaping a sound judgment on the political issues submitted to them, as an equal number of average Masters of Arts and Doctors of Laws, then we should say that the educated man, unless he has been very unlucky with his audience, is perfectly right. He proves that his education has not confined itself to books, bureaux, and an exclusive society, but has been carried on in the bracing air of common life. I will not add anything of my own on this point, because any candidate or member of Parliament is suspect, but I will venture to transcribe a page or so from Mr. Frederic Harrison. Mr. Harrison's intellectual equipment is not inferior to that of Sir Henry Maine himself; and he has long had close and responsible contact with the class of men of whom he is speaking, which cannot be quite a disqualification after all.

No worse nonsense is talked than what we are told as to the requisites for the elective franchise. To listen to some people, it is almost as solemn a function as to be a trustee of the British Museum. What you want in a body of electors is a rough, shrewd eye for men of character, honesty, and purpose. Very plain men know who wish them well, and the sort of thing which will bring them good. Electors have not got to govern the country; they have only to find a set of men who will see that the Government is just and active. . . . All things go best by comparison, and a body of men may be as good voters as their neighbours without being the type of the Christian hero.

So far from being the least fit for political influence of all classes in the community, the best part of the working class forms the most fit of all others. If any section of the people is to be the paramount arbiter in public affairs, the only section competent for this duty is the superior order of workmen. Governing is one thing; but electors of any class cannot or ought not to govern. Electing, or the giving an indirect approval of Government, is another thing, and demands wholly different qualities. These are moral, not intellectual; practical, not special gifts—gifts of a very plain and almost universal order. Such are, firstly, social sympathies and sense of justice; then openness and plainness of character; lastly, habits of action, and a practical knowledge of social misery. These are the qualities which fit men to be the arbiters or ultimate source (though certainly not the instruments) of political power. These qualities the best working men possess in a far higher degree than any other portion of the community; indeed, they are almost the only part of the community which possesses them in any perceptible degree.[1]

The worst of it is that, if Sir Henry Maine is right, we have no more to hope from other classes than from roughs and clowns. He can discern no blue sky in any quarter. 'In politics,' he says, 'the most powerful of all causes is the timidity, the listlessness, and the superficiality of the generality of minds' (p. 73). This is carrying criticism of democracy into

[1] *Order and Progress*, pp. 149-154, and again at p. 174.

an indictment against human nature. What is to become of us, thus placed between the devil of mob ignorance and corruption, and the deep sea of genteel listlessness and superficiality? After all, Sir Henry Maine is only repeating in more sober tones the querulous remonstrances with which we are so familiar on the lips of Ultramontanes and Legitimists. A less timid observer of contemporary events, certainly in the land that all of us know best and love best, would judge that, when it comes to a pinch, Liberals are still passably prudent, and Conservatives quite sufficiently wide-awake.

Another of the passages in Sir Henry Maine's book, that savours rather of the party caricaturist than of the 'dispassionate student of politics,' is the following:

> There is some resemblance between the period of political reform in the nineteenth century and the period of religious reformation in the sixteenth. Now as then the multitude of followers must be distinguished from the smaller group of leaders. Now as then there are a certain number of zealots who desire that truth shall prevail. . . . But behind these, now as then, there is a crowd which has imbibed a delight in change for its own sake, who would reform the Suffrage, or the House of Lords, or the Land Laws, or the Union with Ireland, in precisely the same spirit in which the mob behind the reformers of religion broke the nose of a saint in stone, made a bonfire of copes and surplices, or shouted for the government of the Church by presbyteries (p. 130).

We should wish to look at this picture a little

more closely. That there exist Anabaptists in the varied hosts of the English reformers is true. The feats of the Social Democrats, however, at the recent election hardly convince us that they have very formidable multitudes behind them. Nor is it they who concern themselves with such innovations as those Sir Henry specifies. The Social Democrats, even of the least red shade, go a long way beyond and below such trifles as Suffrage or the Upper House. To say of the crowd who do concern themselves with reform of the Suffrage, or the Land Laws, or the House of Lords, or the Union with Ireland, that they are animated by a delight in change for its own sake, apart from the respectable desire to apply a practical remedy to a practical inconvenience, is to show a rather high-flying disregard of easily ascertainable facts. The crowd listen with interest to talk about altering the Land Laws, because they suspect the English land system of having something to do with the unprosperous condition of the landlord, the farmer, and the labourer; with the depopulation of the country and the congestion in the towns; with the bad housing of the poor, and with various other evils they suppose themselves to see staring them daily in the face. They may be entirely mistaken, alike in their estimate of mischief and their hope of mitigation. But they are not moved by delight in change for its own sake. When the crowd sympathise with disapproval of the House of Lords, it is because the legislative performances of that body are believed to have impeded useful reforms in the past, to be impeding them now, and to be likely to impede them in the future. This may be a sad misreading of the history of the last fifty years, and a painfully prejudiced anticipation of the next fifty. At any rate, it is in intention a solid and practical appeal to experience and results, and has no affinity to a restless love of change for the sake of change. No doubt, in the progress of the controversy, the assailants of the House of Lords attack the principle of birth. But the principle of birth is not attacked from the *a priori* point of view. The whole force of the attack lies in what is taken to be the attested fact that the principle of a hereditary chamber supervising an elective chamber has worked, is working, and will go on working, inconveniently, stupidly, and dangerously. Finally, there is the question of the Irish Union. Is it the English or Scottish crowd that is charged with a wanton desire to recast the Union? Nobody knows much about the matter who is not perfectly aware that the English statesman, whoever he may be, who undertakes the inevitable task of dealing with the demand for Home Rule, will have to make his case very plain indeed in order to make the cause popular here. Then, is it the Irish crowd? Sir Henry Maine, of all men, is not likely to believe that a sentiment which the wisest people of all parties in Ireland for a hundred years have known to lie in the depths of the mind of the great bulk of the Irish population, to whom we have now for the first time given the chance of declaring their wishes, is no more than a gratuitous and superficial passion for change for its own sake. The sentiment of Irish nationality may or may not be able to justify itself in the eye of prudential reason, and English statesmen may or may not have been wise in inviting it to explode. Those are different questions. But Sir Henry Maine himself admits in another connection (p. 83) that 'vague and shadowy as are the recommendations of what is called a Nationality, a State founded on this principle has generally one real practical advantage, through its obliteration of small tyrannies and local oppressions.' It is not to be denied that it is exactly the expectation of this very practical advantage that has given its new vitality to the Irish National movement that seems now once more, for good or for evil, to have come to a head. When it is looked into, then, the case against the multitudes who are as senselessly eager to change institutions as other multitudes once were to break off the noses of saints in stone, falls to pieces at every point.

Among other vices ascribed to democracy, we are told that it is against science, and that 'even in our day vaccination is in the utmost danger' (p. 98). The instance is for various reasons not a happy one. It is not even precisely stated. I have never understood that vaccination is in much danger. Compulsory vaccination is perhaps in danger. But compulsion, as a matter of fact, was strengthened as the franchise went lower. It is a comparative novelty in English legislation (1853), and as a piece of effectively enforced administration it is more novel still (1871). I admit, however, that it is not endured in the United States; and only two or three years ago it was rejected by an overwhelming majority on an appeal to the popular vote in the Swiss Confederation. Obligatory vaccination may therefore one day disappear from our statute book, if democracy has anything to do with it. But then the obligation to practise a medical rite may be inexpedient, in spite of the virtues of the rite itself. That is not all. Sir Henry Maine will admit that Herbert Spencer is not against science, and he expresses in the present volume his admiration for Spencer's work on Man and the State. Spencer is the resolute opponent of compulsory vaccination, and a resolute denier, moreover, of the pretension that the evidence for the advantages of vaccination takes such account of the ulterior effects in the system as to amount to a scientific demonstration. Therefore, if science demands compulsory vaccination, democracy in rejecting the demand, and even if it went further, is at least kept in countenance by some of those who are of the very household of science. The illustration is hardly impressive enough for the proposition that it supports.

Another and a far more momentous illustration occurs on another page (37). A very little consideration is enough to show that it will by no means bear

Sir Henry Maine's construction. 'There is, in fact,' he says, 'just enough evidence to show that even now there is a marked antagonism between democratic opinion and scientific truth as applied to human societies. The central seat in all Political Economy was from the first occupied by the theory of Population. This theory . . . has become the central truth of biological science. Yet it is evidently disliked by the multitude and those whom the multitude permits to lead it.'

Sir Henry Maine goes on to say that it has long been intensely unpopular in France, and this, I confess, is a surprise to me. It has usually been supposed that a prudential limitation of families is rooted in the minds and habits of nearly, though not quite, all classes of the French nation. An excellent work on France, written by a sound English observer seven or eight years ago, chances to be lying before me at the moment, and here is a passage taken almost at random. 'The opinions of thoughtful men seem to tend towards the wish to introduce into France some of that improvidence which allows English people to bring large families into the world without first securing the means of keeping them, and which has peopled the continent of North America and the Australian colonies with an English-speaking race' (Richardson's *Corn and Cattle-Producing Districts of France*, p. 47, etc.). Surely this is a well-established fact. It is possible that denunciations of Malthus may occasionally be found in both

Clerical and Socialistic prints, but then there are reasons for that. It can hardly be made much of a charge against French democracy that it tolerates unscientific opinion, so long as it cultivates scientific practice.

As for our own country, and those whom the multitude permits to lead it, we cannot forget that by far the most popular and powerful man *in fœce Romuli*—as Sir Henry Maine insists on our putting it in that polite way—was tried and condemned not many years ago for publishing a certain pamphlet making a limitation of population the very starting-point of social reform. It is not necessary to pronounce an opinion on the particular counsels of the pamphlet, but the motives which prompted its circulation (motives admitted to be respectable by the Chief Justice who tried the case), and the extraordinary reception of the pamphlet by the serious portion of the workmen of the towns, would make a careful writer think twice before feeling sure that popular bodies will never listen to the truth about population. No doubt, as Sir Henry says in the same place, certain classes now resist schemes for relieving distress by emigration. But there is a pretty obvious reason for that. That reason is not mere aversion to face the common sense of the relations between population and subsistence, but a growing suspicion—as to the reasonableness of which, again, I give no opinion—that emigration is made into an easy and slovenly substitute for a scientific reform in our system of holding and using land. In the case of Ireland, other political considerations must be added.

Democracy will be against science, we admit, in one contingency: if it loses the battle with the Ultramontane Church. The worst enemy of science is also the bitterest enemy of democracy, *c'est le cléricalisme*. The interests of science and the interests of democracy are one. Let us take a case. Suppose that popular government in France were to succumb, a military or any other more popular government would be forced to lean on Ultramontanes. Ultramontanes would gather the spoils of democratic defeat. Sir Henry Maine is much too well informed to think that a clerical triumph would be good for science, whatever else it might be good for. Then are not propositions about democracy being against science very idle and a little untrue? 'Modern politics,' said a wise man (Pattison, *Sermons*, p. 191), 'resolve themselves into the struggle between knowledge and tradition.' Democracy is hardly on the side of tradition.

We have dwelt on these secondary matters, because they show that the author hardly brings to the study of modern democracy the ripe preparation of detail he gave to ancient law. In the larger field of his speculation, the value of his thought is seriously impaired by the absence of anything like a philosophy of society as a whole. Nobody who has studied Burke, or Comte, or Mill—I am not sure whether we should not add even De Maistre—can imagine any of them as setting to work on a general political speculation without reference to particular social conditions. They would have conducted the inquiry in strict relation to the stage at which a community happened to be, in matters lying outside of the direct scope of political government. So, before all other living thinkers, should we have expected Sir Henry Maine to do. It is obvious that systems of government, called by the same name, bearing the same superficial marks, founded and maintained on the same nominal principles, framed in the same verbal forms, may yet work with infinite diversity of operation, according to the variety of social circumstances around them. Yet it is here inferred that democracy in England must be fragile, difficult, and sundry other evil things, because out of fourteen Presidents of the Bolivian Republic thirteen have died assassinated or in exile. If England and Bolivia were at all akin in history, religion, race, industry, the fate of Bolivian Presidents would be more instructive to English Premiers.

One of the propositions that Sir Henry Maine is most anxious to bring home to his readers is that democracy, in the extreme form to which it tends, is of all kinds of government by far the most difficult. He even goes so far as to say (p. 87) that, while not denying to democracies some portion of the advantage that Bentham claimed for them, and 'putting this advantage at the highest, it is *more than compensated* by one great disadvantage,' namely, its difficulty.

This generalisation is repeated with an emphasis that surprises us, for two reasons. In the first place, if the proposition could be proved to be true, we fail to see that it would be particularly effective in its practical bearings. Everybody whose opinions are worth consideration, and everybody who has ever come near the machinery of democratic government, is only too well aware that whether it be far the most difficult form of government or not, it is certainly difficult enough to tax the powers of statesmanship to the very uttermost. Is not that enough? Is anything gained by pressing us further than that? 'Better be a poor fisherman,' said Danton as he walked in the last hours of his life on the banks of the Aube, 'better be a poor fisherman, than meddle with the governing of men.' We wonder whether there has been a single democratic leader either in France or England who has not incessantly felt the full force of Danton's ejaculation. There may, indeed, be simpletons in the political world who dream that if only the system of government were made still more popular, all would be plain sailing. But then Sir Henry Maine is the last man to write for simpletons.

The first reason, then, for surprise at the immense stress laid by the author on the proposition about the difficulty of popular government is that it would not be of the first order of importance if it were true. Our second reason is that it cannot be shown to be true. You cannot measure the relative difficulty of diverse systems of government. Governments are things of far too great complexity for precise quantification of this sort. Will anybody, for example, read through the second volume of the excellent work of M. Leroy-Beaulieu on the Empire of the Czars (1882), and then be prepared to maintain that democracy is more difficult than autocracy? It would be interesting, too, to know whether the Prince on whose shoulders will one day be laid the burden of the German Empire will read the dissertation on the unparalleled difficulties of democracy with acquiescence. There are many questions, of which the terms are no sooner stated than we at once see that a certain and definite answer to them is impossible. The controversy as to the relative fragility, or the relative difficulty, of popular government and other forms of government, appears to be a controversy of this kind. We cannot decide it until we have weighed, measured, sifted, and tested a great mass of heterogeneous facts; and then, supposing the process to have been ever so skilfully and laboriously performed, no proposition could be established as the outcome, that would be anything like adequate reward for the pains of the operation.

This, we venture to think, must be pronounced a grave drawback to the value of the author's present speculation. He attaches an altogether excessive and unscientific importance to form. It would be unreasonable to deny to a writer on democracy as a form of government the right of isolating his phenomenon. But it is much more unreasonable to predicate fragility, difficulty, or anything else of a particular form of government, without reference to other conditions that happen to go along with it in a given society at a given time. None of the properties of popular government are independent of surrounding circumstances, social, economic, religious, and historic. All the conditions are bound up together in a closely interdependent connection, and are not secondary to, or derivative from, the mere form of government. It is, if not impossible, at least highly unsafe to draw inferences about forms of government in universals.

No writer seems to us to approach Machiavelli in the acuteness with which he pushes behind mere political names, and passes on to the real differences that may exist in movements and institutions that are covered by the same designation. Nothing in its own way can be more admirable, for instance, than his reflections on the differences between democracy at Florence and democracy in old Rome—how the first began in great inequality of conditions, and ended in great equality, while the process was reversed in the second; how at Rome the people and the nobles shared power and office, while at Florence the victors crushed and ruined their adversaries; how at Rome the people, by common service with the nobles, acquired some of their virtues, while at Florence the nobles were forced down to seem, as well as to be, like the common people (*Istorie Fiorentine*, bk. iii.).

This is only an example of the distinctions and qualifications which it is necessary to introduce before we can prudently affirm or deny anything about political institutions in general terms. Who would deny that both the stability and the degree of difficulty of popular government are closely connected in the United States with the abundance of accessible land? Who would deny that in Great Britain they are closely connected with the greater or less prosperity of our commerce and manufactures? To take another kind of illustration from Dicey's brilliant and instructive volume on the Law of the Constitution. The governments of England and of France are both of them popular in form; but does not a fundamental difference in their whole spirit and working result from the existence in one country of the *droit administratif*, and the absolute predominance in the other of regular law, applied by the ordinary courts, and extending equally over all classes of citizens? Distinctions and differences of this order go for nothing in the pages before us; yet they are vital to the discussion.

The same fallacious limitation, the same exclusion of the many various causes that co-operate in the production of political results, is to be discerned in nearly every argument. The author justly calls attention to the extraordinary good luck that has befallen us as a nation. He proceeds to warn us that if the desire for legislative innovation be allowed to grow upon us at its present pace—pace assumed to be very headlong indeed—the chances are that our luck will not last. We shall have a disaster like Sedan, or the loss of Alsace-Lorraine (p. 151). This is a curiously narrow reading of contemporary history. Did Austria lose Sadowa, or was the French Empire ruined at Sedan, in consequence of the passion of either of those governments for legislative innovations; or must we not rather, in order to explain these striking events, look to a large array of military, geographical, financial, diplomatic, and dynastic considerations and conditions ? If so, what becomes of the moral ? England is, no doubt, the one great civilised power that has escaped an organic or structural change within the last five-and-twenty years. Within that period, the American Union, after a tremendous war, has revolutionised the social institutions of the South, and reconstructed the constitution. The French Empire has foundered, and a French Republic once more bears the fortunes of a great state over troubled waters. Germany has undergone a complete transformation; so has the Italian peninsula. The internal and the external relations alike of the Austrian Power are utterly different to-day from what they were twenty years ago. Spain has passed from monarchy to republic, and back to monarchy again, and gone from dynasty to dynasty. But what share had legislative innovation in producing these great changes ? No share at all in any one case. What is the logic, then, of the warning that if we persist in our taste for legislative innovation, we shall lose our immunity from the violent changes that have overtaken other states—

changes with which legislative innovation had nothing to do?

In short, modern societies, whether autocratic or democratic, are passing through a great transformation, social, religious, and political. The process is full of embarrassments, difficulties, and perils. These are the dominant marks of our era. To set them all down to popular government is as narrow, as confused, and as unintelligent as the imputation in a papal Encyclical of all modern ills to Liberalism. You cannot isolate government, and judge it apart from the other and deeper forces of the time. Western civilisation is slowly entering on a new stage. Form of government is the smallest part of it. It has been well said that those nations have the best chance of escaping a catastrophe in the obscure and uncertain march before us, who find a way of opening the most liberal career to the aspirations of the present, without too rudely breaking with all the traditions of the past. This is what popular government, wisely guided, is best able to do.

But will wise guidance be endured? Sir Henry Maine seems to think that it will not. Mill thought that it would. In a singularly luminous passage in an essay which for some reason or another he never republished, Mill says—

We are the last persons to undervalue the power of moral convictions. But the convictions of the mass of mankind run hand in hand with their interests or their class feelings. *We have a strong faith, stronger than either politicians or philosophers generally have, in the influence of reason and virtue over men's minds*; but it is in that of the reason and virtue of their own side of the question. We expect few conversions by the mere force of reason from one creed to the other. Men's intellects and hearts have a large share in determining what *sort* of Conservatives or Liberals they will be; but it is their position (saving individual exceptions) which makes them Conservatives or Liberals.

This double truth points to the good grounds that exist why we should think hopefully of popular government, and why we should be slow to believe that it has no better foundation to build upon than the unreal assumptions of some bad philosophers, French, Bolivian, or others.

LIBERALISM AND REACTION.

I.

In the little volume [1] on which I ask leave to offer a few observations, the author, a writer of highly approved competence, asks whether the ideals of the reforming era have lost their efficacy. Have its watchwords ceased to move, is it not true that even the old idols of theatre and market-place have fallen from their pedestals; that an epidemic of unbelief has run through our western world—unbelief in institutions, in principles, churches, parliaments, books, divinities, worst of all, and at the root of all, of man himself? Such epidemics are familiar in the annals of mankind. They are part of the manicheism of human history, the everlasting struggle between the principles of good and evil, and make us think of Luther's comparison of our race to the drunken man on horseback —you no sooner prop him up on one side than he sways heavily to the other. What is the share of democracy in bringing the rider to this precarious and unedifying case? In these high matters let

[1] *Democracy and Reaction.* By L. T. Hobhouse. Fisher Unwin, 1904.

us be sure that nothing is as new as people think. Names are new. Light catches aspects heretofore unobserved. Temperature rises and falls. Yet the elements of the cardinal controversies of human society are few, and they are curiously fixed. Though the ages use ideas differently, the rival ideas themselves hold on in their preappointed courses. Democracy is not new any more than is reaction.

An accomplished Frenchman, now dead, one of the ten thousand critics of democracy, illustrates by a story of his friend Bersot his conviction that human nature will remain to the end pretty like itself, apart from forms of government or measures of social economy. One day Bersot, writing upon Arcachon and its pleasures, wound up his article by saying, 'As for happiness, why there, as everywhere else, you must yourself bring it with you.' So Scherer himself, in like spirit, could not but believe that it is the same with institutions. They depend on what men bring with them. In a less discouraged spirit, or rather with no discouragement of spirit at all, Mr. Hobhouse still recognises that self-government is not in itself a solution of all political and social difficulties. 'It is at best,' he says, ' an instrument with which men who hold by the ideal of social justice and human progress can work, but when those ideals grow cold, it may, like other instruments, be turned to base uses.' The fundamental reform for which the times call is rather a reconsideration of the ends for which all civilised government exists ; in a word, the return to a saner measure of social values. 'We shall be under no illusion,' he concludes, 'about democracy. The golden radiance of its morning hopes has long since faded into the light of common day. Yet, that dry light of noon serves best for those whose task it is to carry on the work of the world.' Reformers are so apt to overlook the truth set out by Tocqueville, when he said that nations are like men, they are still prouder of what flatters their passions than of what serves their interests. Our author's description of the sources and processes by which public opinion in our time is formed, is not lacking in trenchancy, and it might give a pleasure, certainly not intended by its author, to the cynical persons, either at home here or across the Channel, who regard popular government as elaborate dupery, were it not for the author's fervid perception and enforcement of the prime truth, that under every political or social question lies the moral question.

For this sorry transformation he finds four causes. First, he names 'decay in vivid and profound religious beliefs.' This decay was in process a generation ago, but its effects at that time were set off by the rise of a humanitarian feeling which, partly in alliance with the recognised Churches, and partly outside them, took in a measure the place of the old convictions, supplying stimulus and guidance to effort, and yielding a basis for serious and rational public life. These promises have not come true.

A good-natured scepticism has risen up, 'not only about the other world, but also about the deeper problems and higher interests of this.'

If the decay of beliefs is the first element in the reaction against humanitarianism, the second is the diffusion in thought of a stream of German idealism that has swelled the current of retrogression from the plain humanistic rationalistic way of looking on life and its problems.

A third and still more effectual element of reaction has been the career of Prince Bismarck, itself a concrete exemplification of the Hegelian State. 'The prestige of so great an apparent success naturally compelled imitation, and to the achievements of Bismarck, as we are dealing with the forces that have moulded opinion in our own day, we must add the whole series of trials in which the event has apparently favoured the methods of blood and iron, and discredited the cause of liberty and justice.'

After all, however, and this is our fourth cause, 'by far the most potent intellectual support of the reaction has been neither the idealistic philosophy nor the impression made by contemporary events, but the belief that physical science had given its verdict in favour—for it came to this—of violence and against social justice.' In other words, Darwinism. 'But those who have applied Darwin's theories to the science of society have not as a rule troubled themselves to understand Darwin any more than the science of society. What has filtered through into the social and political thought of the time has been the belief that the time-honoured doctrine " Might is Right " has a scientific foundation in the laws of biology. Progress comes about through a conflict in which the fittest survives.'

II.

A French statesman some years ago told a public audience that if a patient linguist, or man of real genius, would only give them a rational dictionary of party appellations, he would earn a statue of fine gold. In the mere strife of party this is not quite certain, for it might happen that too severely rational an investigation of creeds, programmes, and leading persons, and of the precise differences among them, would end, if the dictionary had a great sale, in the disastrous overthrow of many a shrine, and ruin for the political silversmiths who wrought such things. Everybody agrees that whatever else democracy may be, it means in our modern age government by public opinion—the public opinion of a majority armed with a political or social supremacy by the electoral vote, from whatever social classes and strata that majority may be made up. Yet what term in general use is more fluid, elastic, loose? A dozen years before 1832 and the first Reform Bill, Sir Robert Peel spoke of ' the tone of England—of that great compound of folly, weakness, prejudice, wrong feeling, right feeling, obstinacy, and newspaper paragraphs, which is called public opinion.' Yet what statesman has made it the instrument of wiser reforms? In considering, however, a more or less theoretic disquisition like the book before us, we may as well try for clear ideas about our terms. Reaction, for instance, may be only an enemy's name for a new sort of revolution; and some will hold that one crucial subject for England in our day is not democracy and reaction, but democracy and expansion; democracy and the necessities of a vast and heterogeneous empire over sea, how far compatible and reconcilable. Or is our problem at its root, democracy as the antithesis of plutocracy; the form and surface of political power in possession of the many, with all the realities of social power in the grasp of the few? Is this the way in which our case would offer itself to a modern Aristotle, Machiavel, or Montesquieu?

It is no mere platitude that we have reached the threshold of a confused and difficult age. Democracy, nationality, Socialism, the constitution of the modern State, the standing of the Churches—all have come within the attraction of forces heretofore unknown. Science applied to material arts has stimulated production, facilitated transport, multiplied and shortened the channels of communication, made gold as mobile as quicksilver. In different words, the habitable globe has undergone consolidation that only half a century ago would have seemed a miracle. Yet this consolidation, however it may have tended towards liberty and political equality, has by no means tended towards fraternity. The industrial revolution has changed the shape and softened the methods of international rivalry, but hard rivalry remains. It is, again, making civilisation urban, and in England, they say, 70 per cent of our people live in towns. It has, among other cardinal results, magnified by a hundred eyes and arms that power of high finance which has been called 'the most subtle, ubiquitous, and potent of modern political forces.'[1] What passes for public opinion all over Europe is penetrated by unseen, unsuspected, and not over-scrupulous influences. Your Demos, they say, is only a giant marionette, whose wires are pulled from Vienna, Berlin, Paris, New York, the City of London. Demos is not a living creature, with heart, brain, conscience, or even arms and hands to be called its own; it is a puppet of banks and stock-exchanges. This surprising transformation is much more than reaction, much more than simple ebb after flow. Nor can outer changes such as these have swept over the fabric of the world, without carrying changes in their train to match, in all the hopes and fears and aims and affections, in all the catalogue of thoughts on right and duty and relation to extra-mundane things, and the rest of the deep elements on which at last the reality of the individual man is moulded. Here is far more than the mere swing of reaction.

[1] Sir Courtenay Ilbert's *Romanes Lecture on Montesquieu*, p. 40.

All day long we reiterate the question, What is democracy? When we are told, for instance, that the establishment of democracy is the great social fact of the western world between 1830 and, say, 1875, has this been something or nothing more than a political fact? What are the moral bearings of it; can there be a political fact without them? Is democracy only a form of government, or is it a state of society and a name for all those social agencies of which form of government is no more than one? Is it only decentralisation, a shifting of the centre of administrative gravity, or a sublime baptismal conversion to a new faith? Is it only the sovereignty of the people, or one of the secrets of general civilisation? Do you mean simply escape from feudalism, and the establishment of trial by jury, responsibility of the executive, spiritual independence, no taxation without representation? Do you mean a doctrine or a force; constitutional parchment or a glorious evangel; perfected machinery for the wire-puller, the party tactician, the spoilsman, and the boss, or the high and stern ideals of a Mazzini or a Tolstoi?

No answer, at once concise and comprehensive, to this leading question seems attainable. Democracy, said Mazzini, is 'the progress of all through all, under the leadership of the best and the wisest.' The words are eloquent, but every syllable hides a pitfall. The ideal may be exalted and may be just, but the facts of life, of nature, and of history are fatally against it. Are we to seek the democratic principle in Bentham's formula, that 'everybody is to count for one and nobody for more than one'? Are those right who describe the true democratic principle as meaning that none shall have power over the people, and complain that this is perversely taken to mean that none shall be able to restrain or elude the people?

Is democracy another name for Liberalism? Fifty or forty years ago the common superficial answer to this absorbing question would have been Yes. The old school of English politicians to whose memory our author is attached, were not particularly fond of the name of democrat, and even for a time preferred Radical to Liberal. Though the idea and the thing were deeply and primarily English, the use of Liberal as a name for political opinions and political men seems to have come to us from France. Whether in such application it was first devised by Madame de Staël or by Chateaubriand, the books appear unable to decide. Among us the name Liberal in this sense was originally a taunt thrown by Tories against Whigs a century ago. Then it was cheerfully picked up by the judicious Whigs on their own account, as a word of really rather respectable associations than otherwise, just as after the Reform Bill the Tory slowly mellowed himself into Conservative. Signs abound that at no distant day both names may in their turn be superseded; for men, like children, break their toys, and party catchwords, like poems and philosophies, must undergo their fates and fashions.

Some great personages of adventurous mind were by no means sure that democracy means Liberalism. Disraeli did not think so, nor Prince Bismarck; no more, as I should judge, did Cavour. The first of that remarkable trio believed that democracy in England abounded in conservative elements, and the course of events, so well set forth and so acutely analysed in the volume before us, shows that Disraeli did not read the stars amiss. Bismarck never quarrelled with the famous democratic fundamental, that 'governments derive their just powers from the consent of the governed,' nor did he think his own ideal inconsistent with it. 'The ideal,' he said, 'that has always floated before me has been a monarchy that should be so far controlled by an independent national representation — according to my notions, representing classes and callings — that monarch or parliament would not be able to alter the existing statutory position before the law separately, but only *communi sensu*; with publicity and public criticism, by press and Diet, of all political proceedings.' And it has been truly said that Bismarck's story of his relations with Lassalle 'is sufficient proof that he did not discover any ultimate gulf existing between his ideal, and that ideal of a crowned social democracy, which glittered before the imagination of the brilliant Jew.'

We need not, however, go to conservative heroes

either at home or abroad, for proof that liberal and democrat are not identical or co-extensive terms. In more than one time and land the formula of Liberalism has been, '*Everything for the people, nothing by the people.*' The word authoritarian is an ugly word in structure and in signification alike; it only forced or burrowed its way into English a few years ago, and it has been needed to denote that sub-species of the liberal genus, of which Gambetta was the first and most imposing example in our time. A brilliant, learned, versatile French critic once pointed out that Voltaire was the best representative of the French spirit, because he was of all men the most absolutist, and because Liberalism, the opposite of absolutism, is not French. Stirred by the war against clericals and the congregations, M. Faguet in a short book,[1] marked by a keen and searching irony that is characteristic of him, not seldom approaching to splenetic paradox, insists that his countrymen have still to undergo their education in Liberalism. They are all *étatistes*, he declares, accustomed to submit to despotism, eager therefore in turn to practise it; only liberal when they are in a minority, divided between imperious Jacobinism and tyrannical Catholicism. How far all that can be sustained in the facts of the day, this is no occasion to inquire. At least the glowing furnace across the Channel may remind us that, if reaction has been severe in England, democracy has during the same time been going through

[1] *Le Libéralisme.* Émile Faguet (1902).

fiery ordeals in other forms in other places. Democracy, says M. Faguet, is not Liberalism; it is not even liberty; it is parallel, but contradictory. Undoubtedly this is true if we accept some authoritative definitions. Liberalism, according to one Belgian publicist, ' is individualism; it means free examination in the intellectual order, independence in the political order, unlimited expansion of individual activity in the economic order. Its opposite is on one side Socialism, which sacrifices the individual to collectivity; on the other Ultramontanism, that absorbs him in the Church.' [1]

III.

It is on the ideals of the eighteenth century, Mr. Hobhouse assures us, that, say what we may, political Liberalism is founded. That is true, but not without at least one not unimportant qualification. The diplomacy of the three old continental monarchies in the middle years of the eighteenth century was as crooked and as sinister as Europe has ever seen. It was the age of Frederick, Catherine, Kaunitz; and the first partition of Poland is enough to dissipate any dream that the eighteenth century was a golden age of public law and international right. It was not until the final decade that Hope came down

[1] *Réflexions*: Émile Banning (Brussels, 1899), p. 50. Banning took a part in the early stage of Congo affairs, but the King quarrelled with him later.

from heaven to earth—the only blessing that was left behind, after the fatal opening of Pandora's box in Central and Eastern Europe had let loose a cloud of evil torments upon men. Not at once did social hope take its throne in human imagination as the richest solace and inspirer. If we were asked what is the animating faith not only of political liberalism all over the civilised world to-day, but also of hosts of men and women who could not tell us of what school they are, the answer would be that what guides, inspires, and sustains modern democracy is conviction of upward and onward progress in the destinies of mankind. It is startling to think how new is this conviction; to how many of the world's master-minds what to us is the most familiar and most fortifying of all great commonplaces, was unknown. Scouring a library, you come across a little handful of fugitive and dubious sentences in writers of ancient and mediæval time. Bacon's saying, also to be found a long time earlier in Esdras, about antiquity of time being the world's youth, was, as everybody knows, a pregnant hint, but it hardly announced the gospel of progress as now held by most English-speaking persons. Modern belief in human progress had no place among ideals even in the eighteenth century, if we take Voltaire, Montesquieu, Diderot for their exponents; and Rousseau actually thought the history of civilisation a record of the fall of man. Turgot, followed by his faithful disciple Condorcet, first brought into full light, as a governing law of human things, the idea of social progress, moral progress, progress in manners and institutions. It was events, as is their wont, that ripened abstract doctrine into an active moral force. Faith in perfectibility shook for a season faith in authority and tradition and all things established, to its very foundations. After shining in the ascendant in varied phases for the best part of a century or more, the new faith was exposed to the same critical artillery as the old.

What is Progress? It is best to be slow in the complex arts of politics. To hurry to define is rash. If we want a platitude, there is nothing like a definition. Most definitions hang between platitude and paradox. There are said to be ten thousand definitions of Religion. Poetry must count almost as many, and Liberty or Happiness hardly fewer. Define it as we may, faith in Progress has been the mainspring of Liberalism in all its schools and branches. To think of Progress as a certainty of social destiny, as the benignant outcome of some eternal cosmic law, has been indeed a leading Liberal superstition—the most splendid and animated of superstitions, if we will, yet a superstition after all. It often deepens into a kind of fatalism, radiant, confident, and infinitely hopeful, yet fatalism still, and, like fatalism in all its other forms, fraught with inevitable peril, first to the effective sense of individual responsibility, and then to the successful working of principles and institutions of which that responsibility

LIBERALISM AND REACTION.

is the vital sap. Of this fatalism it is not presumptuous to call America the reigning instance at our present time. The young are apt to be too sure. 'Half of history,' said Doudan, 'is made up of unexpected events that force the stream into a different course; and, like one of Mrs. Radcliffe's novels, 'tis at a door hidden in the wall, that the important personages in the drama make their entries and their exits.'

IV.

Like democracy, Liberalism is a name with many shades of meaning, a volume of many chapters. In purpose and aspiration it has undergone a thousand vicissitudes. If some historian were to embark upon the story of Liberalism, where should he begin? The Middle Ages abounded in theories of popular rights with revolutionary applications. The attempt during the Great Schism, and the quarrels of rival popes to establish a sort of parliamentary government by way of periodical councils as the ruling power of the Church[1] proved a failure; but protests against central authority in that transcendent sphere scattered seeds of doubt and revolt over the whole area of government, spiritual and temporal. The Reformation brought the supremacy of prince over people into violent question. The stalwart Levellers in Cromwell's army were strong for law of nature, equality of rights, and the homely pithy doctrine that 'the

[1] See Dr. Law's *Collected Essays and Reviews* (1904), p. 110.

poorest he that is in England hath a life to live as much as the greatest he; and a man is not bound to a government that he has not had a voice to put himself under.' Then came the expulsion of James the Second, and the reasoned vindication of liberal principles from the pen of Locke. But it was the memorable declaration by the American colonists in 1776 that opened the page of the modern democratic evangel—how among self-evident truths are these: That all men are created equal; that they are endowed by their Creator with certain inalienable rights; that among these are life, liberty, and the pursuit of happiness; that, to secure these rights, governments are formed among men, deriving their just powers from the consent of the governed. None of this was new in thought. As American historians point out, Jefferson was here using the old vernacular of English thought and aspiration—a vernacular rich in noble phrase and stately tradition, to be found in a hundred champions of a hundred camps, in Buchanan, Milton, Hooker, Locke, Jeremy Taylor, Roger Williams, and many another humbler but no less strenuous pioneer and confessor of freedom. These were the tributary fountains that, as time went on, swelled into the broad confluence of our modern ages. How great was the debt of Milton or Locke to Jesuit writers—Mariana, Molina, and others under the Spanish crown—we need not here inquire, though the question has an interest of its own. It is circumstance that inspires, selects, and moulds the thought. The commanding novelty in 1776 was the transformation of general thought into a particular polity; of theoretic construction into a working system. Republic became a consecrated and symbolic ensign, carried with torches and flags among the nations. To-day it is hard to imagine any rational standard that would not make the American Revolution—an insurrection of thirteen little colonies with a population of three millions scattered among savages in a distant wilderness—a mightier event in many of its aspects and its effects upon the great wide future of the world, than the volcanic convulsion in France in 1789 and onwards.

The Frenchman would begin his exploration of modern Liberalism with Rousseau. The *Social Contract* (1762) is one of the half-dozen or half-score books that have either wrought, or else announced, revolutions in human thought. By its first vibrating sentence—'Man is born free; yet everywhere he is in chains'—a passionate thrill was sent through that generation and the next. Thirteen years after the portentous document was launched at Philadelphia in 1776, the revolutionists in Paris tried their hands. The French Revolution came. Of no event in history are estimates so various. Some explain it as the upheaval of the Celtic subsoil out of the Roman stratum that formed the overlying arable land, representing wealth, intelligence, energy. To others it is the master-instance of the genius of France, so luminous and so glowing; so combining light with warmth; so full, as Döllinger says, of seductive and penetrating communicability. The French Revolution, cried the trenchant De Maistre comprehensively, has a satanic character. Victor Hugo has boldly contended for the Revolution that it was the greatest step in progress that humanity has made since Christ. Goethe, on the contrary, the supreme intelligence of that age, said: 'We can discern in this monstrous catastrophe nothing but a relentless outbreak of natural forces; no trace of that which we love to signalise as liberty.' Here, too, our island had a share, for it is ideas that matter, and America also had a share. The historical thinker, like Montesquieu, equally with the anti-historical thinker, like Voltaire and Rousseau, both borrowed political ideas, and some ideas deeper than political, from England. Lafayette and Brissot and the Girondists drew their inspiration from the principles that a dozen years before had triumphed in America. 'Ah,' said Marie Antoinette, when the thunderbolts fell around her, ' the time of illusions is past, and we must now pay dear for all our infatuation and enthusiasm for the American war.' Napoleon, while still only Consul, standing at Rousseau's grave in the Isle of Poplars, said, 'It would have been better for the repose of France if this man had never existed. It was he who prepared the French Revolution.' 'I should have thought,' a companion cried, 'that it was not for you of all people to complain of the Revolution.' 'Ah, well,' said Napoleon, 'the future will show whether it would not have been better for the repose of the world, that neither Rousseau nor I had ever existed.'

The declaration of the Rights of Man sprang into flame—the beacon-light of continental Liberalism in Europe ever since. 'The representatives of the people,' said the framers of it, 'constituted as a National Assembly, considering that ignorance, forgetfulness, or contempt of the rights of man, are the only causes of public misfortunes and the corruption of governments, have resolved to set forth in a solemn declaration the natural, inalienable, and sacred rights of man.' Men, they went on, are born free and equal in natural and imprescriptible rights; and these rights are liberty, property, security, and resistance to oppression. Liberty consists in being able to do whatever does not hurt other people, and the limits of natural rights can only be determined by law as distinct from arbitrary power. No set of propositions framed by human ingenuity and zeal has ever let loose more swollen floods of sophism, fallacy, cant, and rant than all this. Yet let us not mistake. The American and French declarations held saving doctrine, vital truths, and quickening fundamentals. Party names fade, forms of words grow hollow, the letter kills; what was true in the spirit lived on, for the world's circumstance needed and demanded it.

After 1815 Liberalism was kept rigorously under, but the fires never died. Bottomless controversies for freedom raged for two or three generations about charters, securities, and guarantees. The questions that for many years held the field in Europe were political—forms of government, details of parliamentary machinery, balance in constitutions, the virtues of suffrage universal or of suffrage limited, the comparative merits of republic and monarchy. The people were to be sovereign. If one state appropriated a piece of territory, a plebiscite was sometimes taken of the wishes of the inhabitants—a recognition of popular principles according to some, by others called mere revolutionary comedy. In Naples in 1820 a revolution was brought to a glorious, joyful, and intoxicating end by the grant of a constitution, of which neither the king who conceded, nor the people who went mad over it, had ever read a word, and about which they knew nothing. This was only one episode in a hundred, of the same struggle, the same intoxication, the same collapse. A whole series of revolts followed in Northern Italy. There was a Spanish revolution, and a Greek insurrection. Then the flame broke out in France in 1830, and there came the three days of Paris, the days of Brussels, the days of Warsaw. Even our steadfast England had its Bristol riots, and the supersession of the landed oligarchy by the ten-pound householder. Over three hundred different constitutions were promulgated in Europe between the years 1800 and 1880. So slow have men been in discovering that the forms of government are much less important than the forces behind them. Forms are only important as they leave liberty and law to awaken and control the energies of the individual man, while at the same time giving its best chance to the common good.

Strange and devious are the paths of history. Broad shining channels get mysteriously silted up; many a time what seemed a glorious high-road, proves no more than a mule-track or mere *cul-de-sac*. Think of Canning's flashing boast, when he insisted on the recognition of the Spanish republics in South America —that he had called a New World into existence, to redress the balance of the Old. This is one of the sayings—of which sort many another might be found —that make the fortune of a rhetorician, yet stand ill the wear and tear of time and circumstance. The New World that Canning called into existence has turned out a scene of singular disenchantment. Though not without glimpses on occasion of that heroism and courage that are the attributes of man almost at the worst, the tale has been a tale of anarchy and disaster, still leaving a host of perplexities for statesmen both in America and in Europe. It has left also to those of a philosophic turn of mind one of the most interesting of all the problems to be found in the whole field of social, ecclesiastical, religious, and racial movement. Why exactly is it that we do not find in the south, as we find in the north of the western hemisphere, a powerful federation, a great Spanish-American people, stretching from the Rio Grande to Cape Horn? To answer that question would be to shed a flood of light upon many deep historic forces in the Old World, of which, after all, these movements of the New are but a prolongation and more manifest extension.

Meanwhile, what passed by the half-mystic name of Revolution, underwent a striking change, and the epoch of nationalities opened. The secret associations of the Carbonari had kept liberal thought and aims in active glow, during the years of Bourbon Restoration in France and of Austrian rule in the Italian Peninsula. The uprising against the yoke of classic tradition in literature was another side of the same liberal movement of men's minds, that made half Europe chafe against the treaties of Vienna and the Holy Alliance. In this uprising, England may be proud to recall, the strength and daring energy of Byron set him among the titanic forces. A passage of Mazzini brings back the spirit of that new era. 'This yearning of the human mind,' he wrote, ' towards an indefinite progress, this force that urges the generations onwards towards the future; this impulse of universal association; the banner of young Europe waving on every side; this varied, multiform, endless warfare everywhere going on against tyranny; this cry of the nations arising from the dust to reclaim their rights, and call their rulers to account for the injustice and oppression of ages; this crumbling of ancient dynasties at the breath of the people; this anathema upon old creeds, this restless search after new; this youthful Europe springing from the old, like the moth from the chrysalis ; this glowing life arising in the midst of death ; this world in resurrection — is not this poetry ? '[1]

Here, and in many another noble word, we hear the accent of romantic democracy in that bygone time. The place of freedom as the moving ideal of liberal schools and parties was taken by the principle of nationality, advanced on behalf not only of Italians, but of Magyars, Greeks, Belgians, Roumanians. The banner of Young Italy, with its colours of white, red, and green, bore on one side the words *Liberty, Equality, Humanity,* and on the other *Unity, Independence.* Such is political metempsychosis in western history, the ceaseless transmigration of the ideals to which men with outstretched hands and straining gaze from age to age make their passionate appeal. Yet diverse meanwhile and vast are the disputable things covered by the alluring name of nationality.

v.

When the French set Europe in a blaze by their Liberty, Equality, and Fraternity, they were nearly all of them thinking of equality in political power. That was to bring the new heaven and the new earth. It was pointed out at an early stage of this vast change in the modern world, that not only equality of right but equality of fact is the real goal of the

[1] *Life and Writings of Mazzini,* i. 152.

social art. Few of the great political insurgencies of history have been unaccompanied by racing economic currents. This is not to say, as Proudhon said, that all revolutions are economic revolutions. For the mightiest changes have come from religious and moral changes in men's hearts. Still, historians have been too prone to underestimate the element of truth in the dictum, ' There is no change in social order without a change in property.' The revolt of the American colonies had its first sources in the restriction by English law of markets for American cotton, tobacco, hides, rice ; the rights of man were like an afterthought. In our own civil war, partly political and still more ecclesiastical, Winstanley and his diggers on St. George's Hill were rude precursors of the socialistic philosophy of to-day. The French Revolution itself was on one side of it a Peasant War. The middle class of Paris and the towns were political, but the countrymen burnt the châteaux and hunted out the landlords for reasons not set out among the rights of man. Even in Paris poor Caius Gracchus Babœuf got many to agree with him that community of goods is the only way of rooting out the egotism that for six thousand years had produced all the crimes and all the sufferings of mortal man. But they cut off his head, and here, as many another time, the blood of martyrs proved *not* to be the seed of the Church.

When the movement of 1830 came, it broke up the confederacy of Europe against the Revolution, planted the system of government by parliaments, and opened the way for socialist and clerical parties.[1] The Revolution of 1848 came, and it wrought deeper than the convulsion of 1789. That was not all. Waving the Red Flag, it alarmed crowned heads all over Europe and shook down thrones. It had ominous inscriptions on its banners. It terrified property. Central and Eastern Europe followed the peoples of the West. Men began to count up the arguments, or shall we say awoke questioning instincts? What is Progress doing for you and me? they asked, and asked more loudly in all lands. Progress may be grand for the shepherds, but what of the sheep? Socialism slowly grew into an aggressive force. In France it came to the birth during the Bourbon Restoration. Louis Philippe coaxed it under. It broke out with furious violence in the days of June. In the reign of Napoleon the Third it slumbered. The crash of Sedan awoke it into fitful activity. To-day it seems to have reached that further stage, long attained in England, when reformers, instead of declaiming on the social question as if it were some single portent overhanging the world, deal with this and that social question in particular.

One of the most ingenious chapters in our short book is an attempt to achieve the reconciliation between Liberalism and Socialism, and to convince us that the breach of principle between them is much smaller than

[1] *Hist. Politique de l'Europe Contemp.*, Seignobos.

might appear upon the surface. Whether the effort amounts to demonstration will be regarded by some as dubious. It is, says Mr. Hobhouse, one of the paradoxes of the reaction that has prevailed for twenty years, that the doctrines of the old Liberalism have lately found some of their staunchest defenders among men who had been wont to look upon most of those doctrines as worn-out platitudes and texts for the obstruction of further progress. In the fight made by the Labour party and the Socialists generally against the South African War, as in the defence of Free Trade, the Socialist leaders and the most notable spiritual descendants of Cobden and Mill stood upon the same platform. Was this alliance, he asks, an accident, or did it arise out of the nature of things, the logical working out of principles in political practice?

He takes a concrete case. Cobden was in favour of prohibiting or restricting the labour of children in a mine or a cotton factory. In this limitation the author discerns two principles. In the first place the child's apparent freedom of contract was not real freedom. In the second it was recognised that the State has a responsibility for, and an interest in, all the conditions that, when operating on a large scale, determine the health and well-being of the community's own members.

Gladstone's famous legislation of 1870 and 1881 again, withdrawing Irish land from the ordinary sphere of contract, furnishes a second example. To say that the Irish cottier was free to make a fair and open bargain with the landlord might be in mere words true, but in relation to the real circumstances it was absurdly untrue.[1] So, adopting the principle that where the necessities of one of the parties to a bargain deprive the seeming freedom of choice of all substance, it is expedient to regulate the bargain by law, Gladstone persuaded Parliament to give the tenant a perpetuity in his holding and to set up a court to fix the rent. I may note in passing, as a point in the history of Liberalism or Democracy or whatever else we call it, that nothing short of Gladstone's own intense readiness of perception, his vast authority, and his extraordinary driving power, could have carried this immense innovation upon the accepted doctrines of free contract and competitive rent, through a Cabinet of landlords, lawyers, and economists. Some, no doubt, viewed the whole operation with the deepest misgivings. The question nearly broke up the Cabinet in 1870, and in 1881 it caused the resignation of the Duke of Argyll—a more definite representative of old-fashioned and current Liberal doctrine than Gladstone ever was. This, however, is by the way; and Mr. Hobhouse is certainly not wrong in saying that where a whole class of men is permanently at a disadvantage in its bargains with another, then by strict Gladstonian principle the State has a right to intervene as arbitrator, provided that it has sufficient equipment of knowledge and impartiality.

[1] See above, pp. 62-69.

VI.

What is certain is, that Socialism appeals to sentiment, raises questions, involves tendencies, and flows over into a vast area, where Liberalism, as ordinarily defined, is hardly likely to feel itself at home, and where Liberalism as a school, moreover, appears in no country in Europe to satisfy either the speculative or the practical tests of its vehement socialising competitor. After all, the more or less of State action is only one point in the contest. So far as that goes, what is curious is that England, where Socialism has as a body of doctrine been least in fashion, has in action carried Socialism in its protective or restrictive aspect further than most other countries. The real issue surely cuts far deeper than this. That issue is at its root the substitution of a new economic system for an old one that was long deemed entirely incontestable. It points to revolution in the relation of workman and capitalist. It tests the foundations of two such venerable pillars of our economic fabric as Rent and Interest. It suggests that the problem of to-day is not production but distribution—a specious form of words that hides a whole crop of fallacies. It involves vital changes in the institution of private property, and in all that enormous and absorbing volume of human thoughts, passions, habits, and aims in life, with which the institution of private property is, and has been for centuries, inextricably associated. It is unhistoric and even anti-historic, and hints that each generation is a law to itself—with some awkward implications for the fund-holder, who makes the tax-payer of to-day ruefully provide money for the ' old unhappy far-off things and battles long ago.' All this stands equally good (or equally evil, if the reader chooses) whether the old view of property be invaded by the storm of social revolution, or more insidiously by the mailed fist of the tax-gatherer and the rate-collector. On this side, too, English democracy has gone, and is going, further in the Socialist direction than foreign communities armed in full panoply of universal suffrage. Our progressive income-tax and death-duties with their sliding scales—the State arbitrarily equalising private fortunes by inequalities of public charge—involve an invasion of the rights of individual property, and therefore of individual liberty, that is up to now rejected both in the French Republic and in the American Republic, and that certainly would have made the men of 1789 and 1793 ' stare and gasp.'

As society grows more complex, calls upon the State wax louder. Yet this very complexity makes intervention more delicate. A generation has passed since Mill, with that patient prescience of his, projected and began a book on Socialism; and in the fragment given to the public [1] he warned his readers that the future of mankind would be gravely imperilled if these great questions were left to be fought over between ignorant change and ignorant opposition

[1] *Fortnightly Review*, 1879.

to change. Since then the discussion has been varied, abundant, tolerably well informed, and in good faith enough to satisfy even Mill, '*si non cum corpore extinguuntur magnæ animæ.*' Nobody was ever more keenly alive than he was to risks of Socialism, and yet he used to say that if the only conceivable alternative were nothing better than the perpetuation of our existing system with its hideous wrong, degradation, and woe, he would face Socialism with all its risks. He did not dream that there is 'any one abuse or injustice now prevailing in society, by merely abolishing which the human race would pass out of suffering into happiness.' What is incumbent upon us, he said, is a calm comparison between the two different systems of society; to see which of them affords the greatest resources for overcoming the inevitable difficulties of life. The world meanwhile revolves in its appointed courses. *Securus judicat.* Improvements are made far less on the strength of this or that abstract principle than under the pressure of social need or exigency, and until the need has come into such light as to rouse and arm the political forces required to overthrow the obstacles. 'Everywhere and always,' said Armand Carrel, 'it is the wants of the time that have created the conventions called political principles, and the principles have always been pushed aside by the wants.'

As for the form of Socialism that is nothing more than wholesale and omnipotent bureaucracy, our author deals with it most faithfully. He perceives that the new cant about 'Efficiency' is little better than the old cant of the good despot, without the good despot's grasp and energy. Liberalism, he says truly, may easily be perverted into an unlovely gospel of commercial competition, in which mutual help is denied as a means of saving the feckless from the consequences of their own character, the impulses of pity are repressed, and self-interest is clothed with the sanctity of a stern duty. Collectivism, on the other hand, has undergone a corresponding perversion on its own account. The liberal and democratic elements are gradually left out, or thrust into obscurity, the free spontaneous moral forces are pooh-poohed, and all the interest is concentrated on the machinery by which life is to be organised. Everything is to fall into the hands of an Expert, who will sit in an office and direct the course of the world. There are some difficulties about the character of the expert.

In the socialistic presentment he sometimes looks strangely like the powers that be—in education, for instance, a clergyman under a new title; in business that very captain of industry who at the outset was the Socialist's chief enemy. Be that as it may, as the Expert comes to the front, and Efficiency becomes the watchword of administration, all that was human in Socialism vanishes out of it. Its tenderness for the losers in the race, its protests against class tyranny, its revolt against commercial materialism, all the sources of the inspiration under which Socialist leaders have faced poverty and prison, are gone like a dream, and instead of them we have the conception of society as a perfect piece of machinery pulled by wires radiating from a single centre, and all men and women are either experts or puppets. Humanity, Liberty, Justice are expunged from the banner, and the single word Efficiency replaces them. Those who cannot take their places in the machine are human refuse, and in the working of a machine there is only one test—whether it runs smoothly or otherwise. What quality of stuff it turns out is another matter. A harder, more unsympathetic, more mechanical conception of society has seldom been devised.

VII.

It has been justly said that the government of Jesuits in Paraguay is the only thing that gives an approximate idea of this bureaucratic Elysium. In truth, argument from abstract principles sounds but a scrannel note in the ears of men and women who have once got into their hearts the famous comparison, in Bellamy's utopian vision, of modern society with ' a prodigious coach, which the masses of humanity were harnessed to, and dragged toilsomely along a very hilly and sandy road'; and how at bad places in the road the desperate straining of the team, their agonised leaping and plunging under the pitiless lashing of hunger, the many who fainted at the rope and were trampled in the mire, ' made a very distressing spectacle which often called forth highly creditable displays of feeling' from the passengers in tolerably easy though precarious seats upon the coach-top.

It is well for us to remember that it is not people lashed by hunger and trampled in the mire who have made revolutions. It has long been well understood that the peasants were less oppressed in France by feudal burdens than in other communities in Europe, and this lightening of the feudal load only rendered the portion of it that was left a hundred times more hateful. For similar reasons any rise in the standard of life tends to quicken discontent that the rise goes no further. So long as it has no root in sour-eyed envy, this discontent itself is a token of progress. I came upon a parable in an interesting American book [1] the other day, of a retired Cape Cod captain, who gave the writer a list of things that entered into the usual consumption of a family sixty years ago. He compared the list with the articles now used in the same neighbourhood. After reflecting, he said, ' My father wanted fifteen things. He got about ten, and worried because he did not get the other five. Now I want forty things, and I get thirty; but I worry more about the ten I can't get, than the old man used to about the five he couldn't get.' Lassalle knew what he was about when he deplored 'the infernal Wantlessness' of men. One clause in any definition of advance in civilisation might be that progress lies in the constant increase in the number of things wanted, in the number of those who want them, and the greater worry if the things wanted

[1] *The Social Unrest*, by John Graham Brooks (New York; Macmillan, 1903).

are not got. What, cries the sceptic, what has become of all the hopes of the time when France stood upon the top of golden hours? Much has come of them, for over the old hopes time has brought a stratum of new.

The share of the Christian religion, and its influence in this wide field of coming innovation, is obscure and doubtful. What is to be the working of the sublime moral revolution nineteen hundred years ago upon the material and mechanical revolution of to-day? The Sermon on the Mount has been reproved by bold critics as bad political economy, and it is unquestionably socialist. Poverty stood high among the early objects of the Christian scheme, but to-day poverty is one of the dead virtues, and the acquisition of property by labour and thrift, like the quiverful of family, is counted as an element of good citizenship. On the latter of these two points the last word has not been spoken, and the question of population dogs our projectors of social regeneration in stealthy ambush. 'It would be possible for the State,' Mill said, to 'guarantee employment at ample wages to all who are born. But if it does this, it is bound in self-protection, and for the sake of every purpose for which government exists, to provide that no person shall be born without its consent.' Only one prominent man, I think, in our time has ventured to touch this dangerous question, and he was sentenced to prison for his pains.

On the chapter of property, for the hour the omens

of stability are sound. Here is what Mr. Roosevelt wrote some years ago :

> There are plenty of ugly things about wealth and its possessors in the present age, and I suppose there have been in all ages. There are many rich people who so utterly lack patriotism, or show such sordid and selfish traits of character, or lead such mean and vacuous lives, that all right-minded men must look upon them with angry contempt ; but, on the whole, the thrifty are apt to be better citizens than the thriftless ; and the worst capitalist cannot harm labouring men as they are harmed by demagogues. As the people of a State grow more and more intelligent, the State itself may be able to play a larger and larger part in the life of the community, while at the same time individual effort may be given freer and less restricted movement along certain lines . . . There may be better schemes of taxation than those at present employed ; it may be wise to devise inheritance taxes, and to impose regulations on the kinds of business which can be carried on only under the especial protection of the State ; and where there is a real abuse by wealth it needs to be, and in this country generally has been, promptly done away with ; but the first lesson to teach the poor man is that, as a whole, the wealth in the community is distinctly beneficial to him ; that he is better off in the long run because other men are well off ; and that the surest way to destroy what measure of prosperity he may have is to paralyse industry and the well-being of those men who have achieved success.[1]

It is interesting, in contrast to such a passage, to recall Macaulay's well-known letter to a gentleman in New York in 1857 : 'The day will come when,

[1] *American Ideals* (1902), pp. 210, 211.

in the State of New York, a multitude of people, none of whom has had more than half a breakfast, or expects to have more than half a dinner, will choose a legislature. Is it possible to doubt what sort of a legislature will be chosen? On one side is a statesman preaching patience, respect for vested rights, strict observance of public faith. On the other is a demagogue ranting about the tyranny of capitalists and usurers, and asking why anybody should be permitted to drink champagne and to ride in a carriage while thousands of honest folks are in want of necessaries? Which of the two candidates is likely to be preferred by a working man who hears his children cry for more bread? . . . There is nothing to stop you. Your constitution is all sail and no anchor.'

Yet amid fierce storm and flood for the years since Macaulay wrote, the American anchor has proved itself no mere kedge. Moral forces decide the strength and weakness of constitutional contrivance. The hunger for breakfast and dinner has not been the master impulse in the history of civilised communities. Selfish and interested individualism has been truly called non-historic. Sacrifice has been the law—sacrifice for creeds, for churches, for kings, for dynasties, for adored teachers, for native land. In England and America to-day the kind of devotion that once inspired followers of Stuarts, Bourbons, Bonapartes, marks a nobler and a deeper passion for the self-governing Commonwealth. Democracy has long passed out beyond mere praise and blame. Dialogues and disputations on its success or failure are now an idle quarrel. Democracy is what it is. Its own perils encompass it. They are many, they are grave. Spiritual power in the old sense there is none ; the material power of wealth is formidable. Like kings and nobles in old time, so in our time, the man in the street will have his sycophants and parasites. At least, as we close Mr. Hobhouse's little book, it is a satisfaction to remember that during these last years of spurious Imperialism in our country, he and other writers of his stamp—instructed, able, diligent, disinterested, and bold—were found to tell both masses and directing classes what they judged to be the truth. This is what the salvation of democracy depends upon.

APHORISMS.[1]

I AM going to ask you to pass a tranquil hour in pondering a quiet chapter in the history of books. One Saturday night last summer I found myself dining with an illustrious statesman on the Welsh border, and on the Monday following I was seated under the acacias by the shore of the Lake of Geneva, where Gibbon, a hundred years ago almost to the day, had, according to his own famous words, laid down his pen after writing the last lines of his last page, and there under a serene sky, with the silver orb of the moon reflected from the waters, and amid the silence of nature, felt his joy at the completion of an immortal task dashed by melancholy that he had taken everlasting leave of an old and agreeable companion. It was natural that I should meditate on the contrast that might be drawn between great literary performance and great political performance, between the making of history and the writing of it—a contrast containing matter enough not only for one, but for a whole series of edifying and instructive discourses. Politics presented difficulties, and I fell back on such book-reflections as

[1] An Address at Edinburgh in 1887.

I could recall on man's busy chase after happiness and wisdom.

What is wisdom? That sovereign word, as has often been pointed out, is used for two different things. It may stand for knowledge, learning, science, systematic reasoning; or it may mean, as Coleridge has defined it, common sense in an uncommon degree; the unsystematic truths that come to shrewd, penetrating, and observant minds, from their own experience of life and their daily commerce with the world, and are called the wisdom of life, or the wisdom of the world, or the wisdom of time and the ages. The Greeks had two words for these two kinds of wisdom: one for the wise who scaled the heights of thought and knowledge; another for those who, without logical method, technical phraseology, or any of the parade of the Schools, whether 'Academics old and new, Cynic, Peripatetic, the sect Epicurean, or Stoic severe,' held up the mirror to human nature, and took good counsel as to the ordering of character and of life.

Mill, in his little fragment on Aphorisms, has said that in the first kind of wisdom every age in which science flourishes ought to surpass the ages that have gone before. In knowledge and methods of science each generation starts from the point at which its predecessor left off; but in the wisdom of life, in the maxims of good sense applied to public and to private conduct, there is, said Mill, a pretty nearly equal amount in all ages.

If this seem doubtful to any one, let him think how many of the shrewdest moralities of human nature are to be found in writings as ancient as the apocryphal Book of the Wisdom of Solomon and of Jesus the Son of Sirach; as Æsop's *Fables*; as the oracular sentences that are to be found in Homer and the Greek dramatists and orators; as all that immense host of wise and pithy saws which, to the number of between four and five thousand, were collected from all ancient literature by the industry of Erasmus in his great folio of Adages. As we turn over these pages of old time, we almost feel that those are right who tell us that everything has been said; that the thing that has been is the thing that shall be, and that there is no new thing under the sun. Even so, we are happily not bound to Schopenhauer's gloomy conclusion (*Werke*, v. 332), that 'The wise men of all times have always said the same, and the fools, that is the immense majority, of all times, have always done the same, that is to say, the opposite of what the wise have said; and that is why Voltaire tells us we shall leave this world just as stupid and as bad as we found it when we came here.'

It is natural that this second kind of wisdom, being detached and unsystematic, should embody itself in the short and pregnant form of proverb, sentence, maxim, and aphorism. The essence of aphorism is the compression of a mass of thought and observation into a single saying. It is the very opposite of dissertation and declamation; its distinction is not so much ingenuity, as good sense brought to a point; it ought to be neither enigmatical nor flat, neither a truism on the one hand, nor a riddle on the other. These wise sayings, said Bacon, the author of some of the wisest of them, are not only for ornament, but for action and business, having a point or edge, whereby knots in business are pierced and discovered. And he applauds Cicero's description of such sayings as salt-pits—that you may extract salt out of them, and sprinkle it where you will. They are the guiding oracles that man has found out for himself in the great business of ours, of learning how to be, to do, to do without, and to depart. Their range extends from prudential kitchen maxims, such as Franklin set forth in the sayings of Poor Richard about thrift in time and money, up to such great and high moralities of life as are the prose maxims of Goethe—just as Bacon's Essays extend from precepts as to building and planting, up to solemn reflections on truth, death, and the vicissitudes of human things. They cover the whole field of man as he is, and life as it is, not of either as they ought to be; friendship, ambition, money, studies, business, public duty, in all their actual laws and conditions as they are, and not as the ideal moralist may wish that they were.

The substance of the wisdom of life must be commonplace, for the best of it is the result of the common experience of the world. Its most universal and important propositions must in a certain sense be truisms. The road has been so broadly trodden by the hosts who have travelled along it, that the main rules of the journey are clear enough, and we all know that the secret of breakdown and wreck is seldom so much an insufficient knowledge of the route, as imperfect discipline of the will. The truism, however, and the commonplace may be stated in a form so fresh, pungent, and free from triviality, as to have all the force of new discovery. Hence the need for a caution, that few maxims are to be taken without qualification. They seek sharpness of impression by excluding one side of the matter and exaggerating another, and most aphorisms are to be read as subject to all sorts of limits, conditions, and corrections.

It has been said that the order of our knowledge is this: that we know best, first, what we have divined by native instinct; second, what we have learned by experience of men and things; third, what we have learned not in books, but by books—that is, by the reflections they suggest; fourth, last and lowest, what we have learned in books or with masters. The virtue of an aphorism comes under the third of these heads: it conveys a portion of a truth with such point as to set us thinking on what remains. Montaigne, who delighted in Plutarch, and kept him ever on his table, praises him in that, besides his long discourses, 'there are a thousand others, that he has only touched and glanced upon, where he only points with his finger to direct us which way we may go if we will, and contents himself sometimes with only giving one brisk hit in the nicest article of the question, from whence we are to grope out the rest.' And this is what Plutarch himself is driving at, when he warns young men that it is well to go for a light to another man's fire, but by no means to tarry by it, instead of kindling a torch of their own.

Grammarians draw a distinction between a maxim and an aphorism, and tell us that while an aphorism only states some broad truth of general bearing, a maxim, besides stating the truth, enjoins a rule of conduct as its consequence. For instance, to say that 'There are some men with just imagination enough to spoil their judgment' is an aphorism. But there is action as well as thought in such sayings as this: ' 'Tis a great sign of mediocrity to be always reserved in praise'; or in this of M. Aurelius, 'When thou wishest to give thyself delight, think of the excellences of those who live with thee; for instance of the energy of one, the modesty of another, the liberal kindness of a third.' Again, according to this distinction of the word, we are to give the name of aphorism to Pascal's saying that 'Most of the mischief in the world would never happen, if men would only be content to sit still in their parlours.'[1] But we should give the name of maxim to the pro-

---

[1] La Bruyère also says: 'All mischief comes from our not being able to be alone; hence play, luxury, dissipation, wine, ignorance, calumny, envy, forgetfulness of one's self and of God.'

found and admirably humane counsel of a philosopher of a very different school, that 'If you would love mankind, you should not expect too much from them.'

The distinction is one without much difference; we need not labour it. Aphorism or maxim, let us remember that this wisdom of life is the true salt of literature; that those books, at least in prose, are most nourishing that are most richly stored with it; and that it is one of the main objects, apart from the mere acquisition of knowledge, which men ought to seek in the reading of books.

A living painter has said, that the longer he works, the more does he realise how very little anybody except the trained artist actually perceives in the natural objects constantly before him; how blind men are to impressions of colour and light and form which would be full of interest and delight, if people only knew how to see them. Are not most of us just as blind to the thousand lights and shades in the men and women around us? We live in the world as we live among fellow-inmates in a hotel, or fellow-revellers at a masquerade. Yet this, to bring knowledge of ourselves and others home to our business and our bosoms, is one of the most important parts of culture.

Some prejudice is attached in generous minds to this wisdom of the world as being egotistical, poor, unimaginative, of the earth earthy. Since the great literary reaction at the end of the eighteenth century, men have been apt to pitch criticism of life in the high poetic key. They have felt with Wordsworth :

> The human nature unto which I felt
> That I belonged, and reverenced with love,
> Was not a punctual presence, but a spirit
> Diffused through time and space, with aid derived
> Of evidence from monuments, erect,
> Prostrate, or leaning towards their common rest
> In earth, the widely-scattered wreck sublime
> Of vanished nations.

Then again, there is another cause for the passing eclipse of interest in wisdom of the world. Extraordinary advances have been made in ordered knowledge of the various stages of the long prehistoric dawn of human civilisation. The man of the flint implement and the fire-drill, who could only count up to five, and who was content to live in a hut like a bee-hive, has drawn interest away from the man of the market and the parlour. The literary passion for primitive times and the raw material of man has thrust polished man, the manufactured article, into a secondary place. All this is in the order of things. It is fitting enough that we should pierce into the origins of human nature. It is right, too, that the poets, the ideal interpreters of life, should be dearer to us than those who stop short with mere deciphering of what is real and actual. The poet has his own sphere of the beautiful and the sublime. But it is no less true that the enduring weight of historian, moralist, political orator, or preacher depends on the amount of the wisdom of life that is hived in his pages. They may be admirable by virtue of other qualities, by learning, by grasp, by majesty of flight; but it is his moral sentences on mankind or the State that rank the prose writer among the sages. These show that he has an eye for the large truths of action, for the permanent bearings of conduct, and for things that are for the guidance of all generations. What is it that makes Plutarch's Lives 'the pasture of great souls,' as they were called by one who was herself a great soul? Because his aim was much less to tell a story than 'to decipher the man and his nature'; and in deciphering the man, to strike out pregnant and fruitful thoughts on all men. Why was it worth while for Jowett to give us a new translation of Thucydides' history of the Peloponnesian War? And why is it worth your while, at least to dip in a serious spirit into its pages? Partly, because the gravity and concision of Thucydides are of specially wholesome example in these days of over-coloured and over-voluminous narrative; partly, because he knows how to invest the wreck and overthrow of those small states with the pathos and dignity of imperial fall; but most of all, for the sake of the wise sentences sown with apt but not unsparing hand through the progress of the story. Well might Gray ask his friend whether Thucydides' description of the final destruction of the Athenian host at Syracuse was not the finest thing he ever read in his life; and assuredly the man who can read that stern tale without admiration, pity, and awe may be certain that he has no taste for noble composition, and no feeling for the deepest tragedy of mortal things. But it is the sagacious sentences in the speeches of Athenians, Corinthians, Lacedæmonians, that do most of all to give the historian his perpetuity of interest to every reader with the rudiments of a political instinct, and make Thucydides as modern as if he had written yesterday.

Tacitus belongs to a different class among great writers. He had, beyond almost any author of the front rank that has ever lived, the art of condensing his thought and driving it home to the mind of the reader with a flash. Beyond almost anybody, he suffered from what a famous writer of aphorisms in our time has described as 'the cursed ambition to put a whole book into a page, a whole page into a phrase, and the phrase into a word.' But the moral thought itself in Tacitus mostly belongs less to the practical wisdom of life than to sombre poetic indignation, like that of Dante, against the perversities of men and the blindness of fortune.

Horace's Epistles are a mine of genial, friendly, humane observation. Then there is none of the ancient moralists to whom the modern, from Montaigne, Charron, Raleigh, Bacon, downwards, owe more than to Seneca. Seneca has no spark of the kindly warmth of Horace; he has not the animation of Plutarch; he abounds too much in the artificial and extravagant paradoxes of the Stoics. But, for all that, he touches the great and eternal commonplaces of human occasion—friendship, health, bereavement, riches, poverty, death—with a hand that places him high among the wise masters of life. All through the ages men tossed in the beating waves of circumstance have found more abundantly in the essays and letters of Seneca than in any other secular writer, words of good counsel and comfort. And let this fact not pass, without notice of the light it sheds on the unity of literature, and of the absurdity of setting a wide gulf between ancient or classical literature and modern, as if under all dialects the partakers in Græco-Roman civilisation, whether in Athens, Rome, Paris, Weimar, Edinburgh, London, Dublin, were not the heirs of a great common stock of thought as well as of speech.

Our own generation in Great Britain has been singularly unfortunate in the literature of aphorism. One too famous volume of proverbial philosophy had immense vogue, but it is so vapid, so wordy, so futile, as to have a place among the books that dispense with parody. Then, rather earlier in the century, a clergyman, who ruined himself by gambling, ran away from his debts to America, and at last blew his brains out, felt peculiarly qualified to lecture mankind on moral prudence. He wrote a little book in 1820, called *Lacon; or Many Things in Few Words, addressed to those who think*. It is an awful example to anybody who is tempted to try his hand at an aphorism. Thus, ' Marriage is a feast where the grace is sometimes better than the dinner.' Finally, a great authoress of our time was urged by a friend to fill up a gap in our literature by composing a volume of Thoughts : the result was that least felicitous of performances, *Theophrastus Such*. One writer of genius has given us a little sheaf of subtly-pointed maxims in the *Ordeal of Richard Feverel*, but he did not divulge to the world the whole contents of Sir Austin Feverel's unpublished volume, *The Pilgrim's Scrip*.

Yet the wisdom of life has its full part in our literature. Keen insight into peculiarities of individual motive, and concentrated interest in the play of character shine not merely in Shakespeare, whose mighty soul, as Hallam says, was saturated with moral observation, nor in the brilliant verse of Pope. For those who love meditative reading on the ways and destinies of men, we have Burton and Fuller and Sir Thomas Browne in one age, and Addison, Johnson, and the rest of the Essayists in another. Sir Thomas Overbury's *Characters*, written in the Baconian age, are found delightful by some ; for my own part, though I have striven to follow the critic's golden rule, to have preferences but no exclusions, Overbury has for me no savour. In the great art of painting moral portraits, or character-writing, the characters in Clarendon, or in Burnet's *History of His Own Time*, are full of life and coherency, and intensely attractive to read. I cannot agree with those who put either Clarendon or Burnet on a level with the characters in St.-Simon or Cardinal de Retz: there is a subtlety of analysis, a searching penetration, a breadth of moral comprehension, in the Frenchmen, which I do not find, nor, in truth, much desire to find, in our countrymen. A homelier hand does well enough for homelier men. Nevertheless, such characters as those of Falkland and Chillingworth, by Clarendon, or Burnet's very different Lauderdale, are worth a thousand battle-pieces, Cabinet plots, or parliamentary combinations of which we never can be sure that the narrator either knew or has told the whole story. It is true that these characters have not the strange quality some one imputed to the writing of Tacitus, that it seems to put the reader himself, and the secrets of his own heart, into the confessional. It is in the novel that, in this country, the faculty of observing social man and his peculiarities has found its most popular instrument. The great novel, not of romance or adventure, but of character and manners, from the mighty Fielding, down at a long interval to Thackeray, covers the field that in France is held, and successfully held, against all comers by her maxim-writers, like La Rochefoucauld, and her character-writers, like La Bruyère. The literature of aphorism contains one English name of immortal lustre—the name of Francis Bacon. Bacon's essays are the unique masterpiece in our literature of this oracular wisdom of life, applied to the scattered occasions of men's existence. The essays are known to all the world;

but there is another and perhaps a weightier performance of Bacon's that is less known, or not known at all except to students here and there. I mean the second chapter of the eighth book of his famous treatise, *De Augmentis*. It has been translated into pithy English, and is to be found in the fifth volume of the great edition of Bacon, by Spedding and Ellis.

In this chapter, among other things, he composes comments on between thirty and forty of what he calls the Aphorisms or Proverbs of Solomon, which he truly describes as containing, besides those of a theological character, 'not a few excellent civil precepts and cautions, springing from the inmost recesses of wisdom, and extending to much variety of occasions.' I know not where else to find more of the salt of common sense in an uncommon degree, than in Bacon's terse comments on the Wise King's terse sentences, and in the keen, sagacious, shrewd wisdom of the world, lighted up by such brilliance of wit and affluence of illustration in the pages that come after them.

This sort of wisdom was in the taste of the time; witness Raleigh's *Instructions to his Son*, and that curious collection 'of political and polemical aphorisms grounded on authority and experience,' which he called by the name of the *Cabinet Council*. Harrington's *Political Aphorisms*, that came a generation later, are more than moral sentences; they are a string of propositions in political theory, breathing a noble spirit of liberty, though too abstract for practical guidance through the troubles of the day. But Bacon's admonitions have a depth and copiousness that are all his own. He says that the knowledge of advancement in life, though abundantly practised, had not been sufficiently handled in books, and so he lays down the precepts for what he calls the *Architecture of Fortune*. They constitute the description of a man who is politic for his own fortune, and show how he may best shape a character that will attain the ends of fortune.

First, A man should accustom his mind to judge of the proportion and value of all things as they conduce to his fortune and ends.

Second, Not to undertake things beyond his strength, nor to row against the stream.

Third, Not to wait for occasions always, but sometimes to challenge and induce them, according to that saying of Demosthenes: 'In the same manner as it is a received principle that the general should lead the army, so should wise men lead affairs,' causing things to be done which they think good, and not themselves waiting upon events.

Fourth, Not to take up anything which of necessity forestalls a great quantity of time, but to have this sound ever ringing in our ears: 'Time is flying—time that can never be retrieved.'

Fifth, Not to engage one's-self too peremptorily in anything, but ever to have either a window open to fly out at, or a secret way to retire by.

Sixth, To follow that ancient precept, not construed to any point of perfidiousness, but only to caution and moderation, that we are to treat our friend as if he might one day be a foe, and our foe as if he should one day be a friend.

All these Bacon called the good arts, as distinguished from the evil arts that had been described years before by Machiavelli in his famous book *The Prince*, and also in his *Discourses*. Bacon called Machiavelli's sayings depraved and pernicious, and a corrupt wisdom, as indeed they are. He was conscious that his own maxims, too, stood in some need of elevation and of correction, for he winds up with wise warnings against being carried away by a whirlwind or tempest of ambition; by the general reminder that all things are vanity and vexation of spirit, and the particular and most profound reminder that 'All virtue is most rewarded, and all wickedness most punished, in itself'; by the question whether this incessant, restless, and, as it were, Sabbathless pursuit of fortune, leaves time for holier duties, and what advantage it is to have a face erected towards heaven, with a spirit perpetually grovelling upon earth, eating dust like a serpent; and finally, he says that it will not be amiss for men, in this eager and excited chase of fortune, to cool themselves a little with that conceit of Charles V. in his instructions to his son, that 'Fortune hath somewhat of the nature of a woman, who, if she be too closely wooed, is commonly the further off.'

There is Baconian humour as well as a curious

shrewdness in such an admonition as that which I will here transcribe, and there are many like it:

> It is therefore no unimportant attribute of prudence in a man to be able to set forth to advantage before others, with grace and skill, his virtues, fortunes, and merits (which may be done without arrogance or breeding disgust); and again, to cover artificially his weaknesses, defects, misfortunes, and disgraces; dwelling upon the former and turning them to the light, sliding from the latter or explaining them away by apt interpretations and the like. Tacitus says of Mucianus, the wisest and most active politician of his time, 'That he had a certain art of setting forth to advantage everything he said or did.' And it requires indeed some art, lest it become wearisome and contemptible; but yet it is true that ostentation, though carried to the first degree of vanity, is rather a vice in morals than in policy. For as it is said of calumny, 'Calumniate boldly, for some of it will stick,' so it may be said of ostentation (except it be in a ridiculous degree of deformity), 'Boldly sound your own praises, and some of them will stick.' It will stick with the more ignorant and the populace, though men of wisdom may smile at it; and the reputation won with many will amply countervail the disdain of a few. . . . And surely no small number of those who are of a solid nature, and who, from the want of this ventosity, cannot spread all sail in pursuit of their own honour, suffer some prejudice and lose dignity by their moderation.

Such writings as these may have no place in that nobler literature, from Epictetus and Marcus Aurelius downwards, which lights up the young soul with generous aims, and fires it with the love of all excellence. Yet the most heroic cannot do without a dose of circumspection. The counsels of old Polonius to Laertes are less sublime than Hamlet's soliloquy, but they have their place. Bacon's chapters are a manual of circumspection, whether we choose to give to circumspection a high or a low rank in the list of virtues. Bacon knew of the famous city that had three gates, and on the first the horseman read inscribed, 'Be bold'; and on the second gate yet again, 'Be bold, and evermore be bold'; and on the third it was written, 'Be not too bold.'

This cautious tone had been brought about by the circumstances of the time. Government was strict; dissent from current opinions was dangerous; there was no indifference and hardly any tolerance; authority was suspicious and it was vindictive. When the splendid genius of Burke rose like a new sun into the sky, the times were happier, and nowhere in our literature does a noble prudence wear statelier robes than in the majestic compositions of Burke.

Those who are curious to follow the literature of aphorism into Germany, will, with the mighty exceptions of Goethe and Schiller, find but a parched and scanty harvest. The Germans too often justify the unfriendly definition of an aphorism as a form of speech wrapping up something quite plain, in words that turn it into something very obscure. As old Fuller says, the writers have a hair hanging to the nib of their pen. Their shortness does not prevent them from being tiresome. They recall the

French wit to whom a friend showed a distich: 'Excellent,' he said; 'but rather spun out.'

Lichtenberg, a professor of physics, who was also a considerable hand at satire a hundred years ago, composed a collection of sayings, not without some wheat amid much chaff. A later German writer, Schopenhauer, has some excellent remarks on Self-reflection, and on the difference between those who think for themselves and those who think for other people; between genuine Philosophers, who look at things first hand for their own sake, and Sophists, who look at words and books for the sake of making an appearance before the world, and seek their happiness in what they hope to get from others: he takes Herder for an example of the Sophist, and Lichtenberg for the true Philosopher. It is true that we hear the voice of the Self-thinker, and not the mere Book-philosopher, if we may use for once those uncouth compounds, in such sayings as these:

People who never have any time are the people who do least.

The utmost that a weak head can get out of experience is an extra readiness to find out the weaknesses of other people.

Over-anxiously to feel and think what one could have done, is the very worst thing one can do.

He who has less than he desires, should know that he has more than he deserves.

Enthusiasts without capacity are the really dangerous people.

Radowitz was a Prussian soldier and statesman,

who died in 1853, after doing enough to convince men that the Revolution of 1848 produced no finer mind. He left among other things two or three volumes of short fragmentary pieces on politics, religion, literature, and art. They are intelligent and elevated, but contain hardly anything to our point to-night, unless it be this,—that what is called Stupidity springs not at all from mere want of understanding, but from the fact that the free use of a man's understanding is hindered by some definite vice: Frivolity, Envy, Dissipation, Covetousness, all these darling vices of fallen man,—these are at the bottom of what we name Stupidity. This is true enough, but it is not so much to the point as the saying of a highly judicious aphorist of my own acquaintance, that 'Excessive anger against human stupidity is itself one of the most provoking of all forms of stupidity.'

Another author of aphorisms of Goethe's period was Klinger, a playwriter, who led a curious and varied life in camps and cities. He began with a vehement enthusiasm for the sentimentalism of Rousseau, and ended, as such men often end, with a hard and stubborn cynicism. He wrote *Thoughts on different Subjects of the World and Literature*, which are intelligent and masculine, if they are not particularly pungent in expression. One of them runs—'He who will write interestingly must be able to keep heart and reason in close and friendliest connection. The heart must warm the reason, and reason must in turn blow on the embers if they are to burst into flame.' This illustrates what an aphorism should not be. Contrast its clumsiness with the brevity of the admirable saying of Vauvenargues, that 'Great thoughts come from the heart.'

Schopenhauer gave to one of his minor works the name of *Aphorismen zu Lebens-Weisheit,* ' Aphorisms for the Wisdom of Life,' and he put to it, by way of motto, Chamfort's saying, ' Happiness is no easy matter; 'tis very hard to find it within ourselves, and impossible to find it anywhere else.' Schopenhauer was so well read in European literature, he had such natural alertness of mind, and his style is so pointed, direct, and wide-awake, that these detached discussions are interesting and most readable; but for the most part they are discussions and not aphorisms. The whole collection, winding up with the chapter of Counsels and Maxims, is in the main an unsystematic enforcement of those peculiar views of human happiness and its narrow limits that proved to be the most important part of Schopenhauer's system. ' The sovereign rule in the wisdom of life,' he said, ' I see in Aristotle's proposition (*Eth. Nic.* vii. 12), ὁ φρόνιμος τὸ ἄλυπον διώκει, οὐ τὸ ἡδύ: Not pleasure, but freedom from pain is what the sensible man seeks after.' The second volume, of Detached though systematically Ordered Thoughts on Various Circumstances, is miscellaneous in its range of topics, and is full of suggestion; but the thoughts are mainly philosophical and literary, and do not come very close to practical wisdom. In truth, so negative a view of happiness, such pale hopes and middling expectations, could not guide a man far on the path of active prudence, where we naturally take for granted that the goal is really something substantial, serious, solid, and positive.[1]

Nobody cared less than Schopenhauer for the wisdom that is drawn from books, or has said such hard things of mere reading. In the short piece to which I have already referred (p. 171), he works out the difference between the Scholar who has read in books, and the Thinkers, the Geniuses, the Lights of the World, and Furtherers of the human race, who have read directly from the world's own pages. Reading, he says, is only a *succedaneum* for one's own thinking. Reading is thinking with a strange head instead of one's own. People who get their wisdom out of books are like those who have got their knowledge of a country from the descriptions of travellers. Truth that has been picked up from books only sticks to us like an artificial limb, or a false tooth, or a

[1] Burke says on the point raised above: 'I am satisfied the ideas of pain are much more powerful than those which enter on the part of pleasure. Without all doubt, the torments which we may be made to suffer are much greater in their effect on the body and mind, than any pleasures which the most learned voluptuary could suggest. Nay, I am in great doubt whether any man could be found, who would earn a life of the most perfect satisfaction at the price of ending it in the torments which justice inflicted in a few hours on the late unfortunate regicide in France' (*Sublime and Beautiful*, pt. i. sec. vii.). The reference is, of course, to Damiens.

rhinoplastic nose; the truth we have acquired by our own thinking is like the natural member. At least, as Goethe puts it in his verse,

> Was du ererbt von deinen Vätern hast,
> Erwirb es, um es zu besitzen.

What from thy fathers thou dost inherit, be sure thou earn it, that so it may become thine own.

It is only Goethe and Schiller, and especially Goethe, 'the strong, much-toiling sage, with spirit free from mists, and sane and clear,' who combine the higher and the lower wisdom, and have skill to put moral truths into forms of words that fix themselves with stings in the reader's mind. All Goethe's work, whether poetry or prose, his plays, his novels, his letters, his conversations, are richly bestrewn with the luminous sentences of a keen-eyed, steadfast, patient, indefatigable watcher of human life. He deals gravely and sincerely with men. He has none of the shallow irony by which small men who have got wrong with the world seek a shabby revenge. He tells us the whole truth. He is not of those second-rate sages who keep their own secrets, externally complying with all the conventions of speech and demeanour, while privately nourishing unbridled freedom of opinion in the inner sanctuary of the mind. He handles soberly, faithfully, laboriously, cheerfully, every motive and all conduct. He marks himself the friend, the well-wisher, and the helper. I will not begin to quote from Goethe, for

I should never end. The volume of *Sprüche*, or aphorisms in rhyme and prose in his collected works, is accessible to everybody, but some of his wisest and finest are to be found in the plays, like the well-known one in his *Tasso*, ' In stillness Talent forms itself, but Character in the great current of the world.'

But here is a concentrated admonition from the volume I have named, that will do as well as any other for an example of his temper—

> Wouldst fashion for thyself a seemly life ?—
> Then fret not over what is past and gone ;
> And spite of all thou mayst have lost behind,
> Yet act as if thy life were just begun.
> What each day wills, enough for thee to know ;
> What each day wills, the day itself will tell.
> Do thine own task, and be therewith content ;
> What others do, that shalt thou fairly judge ;
> Be sure that thou no brother-mortal hate,
> Then all besides leave to the Master Power.

It is France that excels in the form no less than in the matter of aphorism, for the good reason that in France the arts of polished society were relatively at an early date the objects of a serious and deliberate cultivation, such as was, and perhaps remains, unknown in the rest of Europe. Conversation became a fine art. ' I hate war,' said one ; ' it spoils conversation.' The leisured classes found their keenest relish in delicate irony, in piquancy, in contained vivacity, in the study of niceties of observation and finish of phrase. You have a picture of it in such a play as Molière's *Misanthropist*, where we see a section of the polished life of the time—men and women making and receiving compliments, discoursing on affairs with easy lightness, flitting backwards and forwards with a thousand petty hurries, and among them one singular figure, hoarse, rough, sombre, moving with a chilling reality in the midst of frolic and shadows. But the shadows were all in all to one another. Not a point of conduct, not a subtlety of social motive, escaped detection and remark.

Dugald Stewart has pointed to the richness of the French tongue in appropriate and discriminating expressions for varieties of intellectual turn and shade. How many of us, who claim to a reasonable knowledge of French, will undertake easily to find English equivalents for such distinctions as are expressed in the following phrases—*Esprit juste, esprit étendu, esprit fin, esprit délié, esprit de lumière.* These numerous distinctions are the evidence, as Stewart says, of the attention paid by the cultivated classes to delicate shades of mind and feeling. Compare with them the colloquial use of our terribly overworked word 'clever.' Society and conversation have hardly been among us the spring of literary inspiration they have been in France. The English rule has rather been like that of the ancient Persians, that the great thing is to learn to ride, to shoot with the bow, and to speak the truth. There is much in it. But it has been more favourable to strength than to either subtlety or finish.

One of the most commonly known of all books of maxims, after the Proverbs of Solomon, is the *Moral Reflections* of La Rochefoucauld. The author lived at court, himself practised all the virtues which he seemed to disparage, and took so much trouble to make sure of the right expression that many of these short sentences were more than thirty times revised. They were given to the world in the last half of the seventeenth century in a little volume that Frenchmen used to know by heart; it gave a new turn to the literary taste of the nation, and has been translated into every civilised tongue. It paints men as they would be if self-love were the one great mainspring of human action, and it makes magnanimity itself no better than self-interest in disguise.

We cannot wonder that in spite of their piquancy of form, such sentences have aroused in many minds an invincible repugnance for what would be so tremendous a calumny on human nature, if the book were meant to be a picture of human nature as a whole. 'I count Rochefoucauld's *Maxims*,' says one critic, 'a bad book. As I am reading it, I feel discomfort; I have a sense of suffering which I cannot define. Such thoughts tarnish the brightness of the soul; they degrade the heart.' Yet as a faithful presentation of human selfishness, and of you and me in so far as we happen to be mainly selfish, the odious mirror has its uses by showing us what manner of man we are or may become. Let us not forget either that not quite all is selfishness in La Rochefoucauld.

Everybody knows his saying that hypocrisy is the homage vice pays to virtue. There is a subtle truth in this, too,—that to be in too great a hurry to discharge an obligation is itself a kind of ingratitude. Nor is there any harm in the reflection that no fool is so troublesome as the clever fool; nor in this, that only great men have any business with great defects; nor, finally, in the consolatory saying, that we are never either so happy or so unhappy as we imagine.

No more important name is associated with the literature of aphorism than that of Pascal; but the *Thoughts* of Pascal concern the deeper things of speculative philosophy and religion, rather than the wisdom of daily life, and, besides, though aphoristic in form, they are in substance systematic. 'I blame equally,' he said, 'those who take sides for praising man, those who are for blaming him, and those who amuse themselves with him : the only wise part is search for truth—search with many sighs.' On man, as he exists in society, he said little; and what he said does not make us hopeful. He saw the darker side. 'If everybody knew what one says of the other, there would not be four friends left in the world.' 'Would you have men think well of you, then do not speak well of yourself.' If you wish to know Pascal's theory you may find it set out in brilliant verse in the opening lines of the second book of Pope's *Essay on Man*. 'What a chimera is Man!' said Pascal. 'What a confused chaos! What a subject of contradiction! A professed judge of all

things, and yet a feeble worm of the earth; the great
depository and guardian of truth, and yet a mere
huddle of uncertainty; the glory and the scandal of
the universe.' Shakespeare was wiser and deeper
when, under this quintessence of dust, he discerned
what a piece of work is man, how noble in reason,
how infinite in faculty, in form and moving how
express and admirable. That serene and radiant
faith is the secret, added to matchless gifts of imagination and music, of Shakespeare's being the greatest
of men.

There is a smart, spurious wisdom of the world
which has the bitterness not of the salutary tonic but
of mortal poison; and of this kind the master is
Chamfort, who died during the French Revolution
(and, for that matter, died of it), and whose little
volume of thoughts is often extremely witty, always
pointed, but not seldom cynical and false. 'If you
live among men,' he said, 'the heart must either
break or turn to brass.' 'The public, the public,'
he cried; 'how many fools does it take to make a
public!' 'What is celebrity? The advantage of
being known to people who don't know you.'

We cannot be surprised to hear of the lady who
said that a conversation with Chamfort in the morning
made her melancholy until bedtime. Yet Chamfort
is the author of the not unwholesome saying that
'The most wasted of all days is that on which one
has not laughed.' One of his maxims lets us into
the secret of his misanthropy. 'Whoever,' he said,

'is not a misanthropist at forty can never have loved mankind.' It is easy to know what this means. Of course if a man is so superfine that he will not love mankind any longer than he can believe them to be demigods and angels, it is true that at forty he may have discovered that they are neither. Beginning by looking for men to be more perfect than they can be, he ends by thinking them worse than they are, and then he secretly plumes himself on his superior cleverness in having found humanity out. For the deadliest of all wet blankets give me a middle-aged man who has been most of a visionary in his youth.

Let us remember that Fénelon, one of the most saintly of men, whose very countenance bore such a mark of goodness that when he was in a room men found they could not desist from looking at him, wrote to a friend the year before he died, 'I ask little from most men; I try to render them much, and to expect nothing in return, and I get very well out of the bargain.'

Chamfort I will leave, with his sensible distinction between Pride and Vanity. 'A man,' he says, 'has advanced far in the study of morals who has mastered the difference between pride and vanity. The first is lofty, calm, immovable; the second is uncertain, capricious, unquiet. The one adds to a man's stature; the other only puffs him out. The one is the source of a thousand virtues; the other is that of nearly all vices and all perversities. There is a kind of pride in which are included all the commandments of God; and a kind of vanity which contains the seven mortal sins.'

I will say little of La Bruyère—by far the greatest, broadest, strongest, of French character-writers,— because his is not one of the houses of which you can judge by a brick or two taken at random. For those in whom the excitements of modern literature have not burnt up the faculty of sober meditation on social man, La Bruyère must always be one of the foremost names. Macaulay somewhere calls him thin. But then, Macaulay is not at his strongest in ethical depth, in perception of ethical depth, in proportion to his manly and brilliant gifts in other ways; and *thin* is the very last word that describes this admirable master. We feel that La Bruyère, though retiring, studious, meditative, and self-contained, has complied with the essential condition of looking at life and men themselves, and with his own eyes. His aphoristic sayings are the least important part of him, but here are one or two examples:

Eminent posts make great men greater, and little men less.

There is in some men a certain mediocrity of mind that helps to make them wise.

The flatterer has not a sufficiently good opinion either of himself or of others.

People from the provinces and fools are always ready to take offence, and to suppose that you are laughing at them: we should never risk a pleasantry, except with well-bred people, and people with brains.

All confidence is dangerous, unless it is complete:

there are few circumstances in which it is not best either to hide all or to tell all.

When the people is in a state of agitation, we do not see how quiet is to return ; and when it is tranquil, we do not see how the quiet is to be disturbed.

Men count for almost nothing the virtues of the heart, and idolise gifts of body or intellect. The man who quite coolly, and with no idea that he is offending modesty, says that he is kind-hearted, constant, faithful, sincere, fair, grateful, would not dare to say that he is quick and clever, that he has fine teeth and a delicate skin.

I will say nothing of Rivarol, a caustic wit of the revolutionary time, nor of Joubert, a writer of sayings of the nineteenth century, of whom Matthew Arnold has said all that needs saying. He is delicate, refined, acute, but his thoughts were fostered in the hothouse of a coterie, and have none of the salt and sapid flavour that comes to more masculine spirits from active contact with the world.

I should prefer to close this survey in the sunnier moral climate of Vauvenargues. His own life was a pathetic failure in all the aims of outer circumstance. The chances of fortune and of health persistently baulked him, but from each stroke he rose up again, with undimmed serenity and undaunted spirit. As blow fell upon blow, the sufferer held firmly to his incessant lesson,—Be brave, persevere in the fight, struggle on, do not let go, think magnanimously of man and life, for man is good and life is affluent and fruitful. He died over a hundred and fifty years ago, leaving a little body of maxims behind him which, for tenderness, equanimity, cheerfulness, grace, sobriety, and hope, are not surpassed in prose literature. He well deserves, and shall have, a chapter of his own.

The best-known of Vauvenargues' sayings, as it is the deepest and the broadest, is the far-reaching sentence so often, but none too often, quoted, that 'Great thoughts come from the heart.' And this is the truth that shines out as we watch the voyagings of humanity from the 'wide, grey, lampless depths' of time. Those have been greatest in thought who have been best endowed with faith, hope, sympathy, and the spirit of effort. And next to them come the great stern men, like Tacitus, Dante, Pascal, who, standing as far aloof from the soft poetic dejection of some of the moods of Shelley or Keats as from the savage fury of Swift, watch with a prophet's indignation the heedless waste of faculty and opportunity, the triumph of paltry motive and paltry aim, as if we were the flies of a summer noon, which do more than any active malignity to distort the noble lines, and to weaken or to frustrate the strong and healthy parts, of human nature. For practical purposes all these complaints of man are of as little avail as Johnson found the complaint that so large a space of the globe should be occupied by the uninhabitable ocean, encumbered by naked mountains, lost under barren sands, scorched by perpetual heat or petrified by perpetual frost, and so small a space be left for the production of fruits, the pasture of cattle, and the accommodation of men.

When we have deducted, said Johnson, all the time that is absorbed in sleep, or appropriated to other demands of nature, or the inevitable requirements of social intercourse, all that is torn from us by violence of disease, or imperceptibly stolen from us by languor, we may realise of how small a portion of our time we are truly masters. And the same consideration of the ceaseless and natural preoccupations of men in the daily struggle will reconcile the wise man to all the disappointments, delays, shortcomings of the world, without shaking his own faith or his own purpose.

VAUVENARGUES.

ONE of the most important phases of French thought in the century of its illumination is only intelligible on condition that in studying it we keep constantly in mind the eloquence, force, and genius of Pascal. He was the greatest and most influential representative of that way of viewing human nature and its circumstances against which it was one of the glories of the eighteenth century to have rebelled. More than a hundred years after the publication of the *Pensées*, Condorcet thought it worth while to prepare a new edition of them, with annotations, protesting, not without a certain unwonted deference of tone, against Pascal's doctrine of the base and desperate estate of man. Voltaire also had them reprinted with notes of his own, written in the same spirit of vivacious deprecation, that we may be sure would have been even more vivacious, if Voltaire had not remembered that he was speaking in Pascal of the mightiest of all the enemies of the Jesuits. Apart from formal and specific dissents like these, all the writers who had drunk most deeply of the spirit of the eighteenth century, lived in a constant ferment of revolt against the clear-witted and vigorous thinker of the century before, who had clothed theological mysteries with the force and importance of strongly entrenched propositions in a consistent philosophic scheme.

The resplendent fervour of Bossuet's declamations upon the nothingness of kings, the pitifulness of mortal aims, the crushing ever-ready grip of the hand of God upon the purpose and faculty of man, rather filled the mind with exaltation than really depressed or humiliated it. From Bossuet to Pascal is to pass from the solemn splendour of the church to the chill of the crypt. Besides, Bossuet's attitude was professional, in the first place, and it was purely theological, in the second; so the main stream of thought flowed away and aside from him. To Pascal it was felt necessary that there should be reply and vindication, whether in the shape of deliberate and published formulas, or in the reasoned convictions of the individual intelligence working privately. A syllabus of the radical articles of the French creed of the eighteenth century would consist largely of the contradictories of the main propositions of Pascal. The old theological idea of the fall was hard to endure, but the idea of the fall was clenched by such general laws of human nature as this,—that 'men are so necessarily mad, that it would be to be mad by a new form of madness not to be mad';—that man is nothing but masquerading, lying, and hypocrisy, both in what concerns himself and in respect of others, wishing not to have the truth told to himself, and shrinking from telling it to anybody else;[1] that the will, the imagination, the disorders of the body, the thousand concealed infirmities of the intelligence, conspire to reduce our discovery of justice and truth to a process of haphazard, in which we more often miss the mark than hit.[2] Pleasure, ambition, industry, are only means of distracting men from the otherwise unavoidable contemplation of their own misery. How speak of the dignity of the race and its history, when we know that a grain of sand in Cromwell's bladder altered the destinies of a kingdom, and that if Cleopatra's nose had been shorter the whole surface of the earth would be different? Imagine, in a word, 'a number of men in chains, and all condemned to death; some of them each day butchered in the sight of the others, while those who remain watch their own condition in that of their fellows, and eyeing one another in anguish and despair, wait their turn; such is the situation of man.'[3]

It was hardly possible to force the tragical side of a life's verities beyond this, and there was soon an instinctive reaction towards realities. The sensations with their conditions of pleasure no less than of pain; the intelligence with its energetic aptitudes for the discovery of fruitful and protective knowledge; the affections with their large capacities for giving and receiving delight; the spontaneous inner impulse

[1] *Pensées*, I. v. 8.   [2] *Ibid.* I. vi. 16.
[3] *Ibid.* I. vii. 6.

towards action and endurance in the face of outward circumstances—all these things reassured men, and restored to them in theory with ample interest what in practice they had never lost—a rational faith and exultation in their own faculties, both of finding out truth and of feeling a substantial degree of happiness. On this side too, as on the other, speculation went to its extreme limit. The hapless and despairing wretches of Pascal were transformed by the votaries of perfectibility into bright beings not any lower than the angels. Between the two extremes there was one fine moralist who knew how to hold a just balance, perceiving that language is the expression of relations and proportions, that when we speak of virtue and genius, we mean qualities that, compared with those of mediocre souls, deserve these high names; that greatness and happiness are comparative terms, and that there is nothing to be said of the estate of man except relatively. This moralist was Vauvenargues.

Vauvenargues was born of a good Provençal stock at Aix, in the year 1715. He had scarcely any of that kind of education which is usually performed in school-classes, and he was never able to read either Latin or Greek. Such slight knowledge as he ever got of the famous writers among the ancients was in translations. Of English literature, though its influence and that of our institutions were then becoming paramount in France, and though he had a particular esteem for the English character, he knew only the writings of Locke and Pope, and *Paradise*

Lost.[1] Vauvenargues must be added to the list of thinkers and writers whose personal history shows, what men of letters sometimes appear to be in a conspiracy to make us forget, that for sober, healthy, and robust judgment on human nature and life, active and sympathetic contact with men in the transaction of the many affairs of their daily life is a better preparation than any amount of wholly meditative seclusion. He is also one of the many who show that a weakly constitution of body is not incompatible with fine and energetic qualities of mind, even if it be not actually friendly to them. Nor was indifferent health any disqualification for the profession of arms. As Arms and the Church were the only alternatives for persons of noble birth, Vauvenargues, choosing the former, became a subaltern in the King's Own Regiment at the age of twenty (1735). Here in time he saw active service; for in 1740 the death of Charles VI. threw all Europe into confusion, and the French government, falling in with the prodigious designs of Marshal Belle-Isle and his brother, took sides against Maria Theresa, and supported the claims of the unhappy Elector of Bavaria who afterwards became the Emperor Charles VII. The disasters that fell upon France in consequence are well known. The forces despatched to Bavaria and Bohemia, after the brief triumph of the capture of Prague, were gradually overwhelmed

---

[1] M. Gilbert's edition of the *Works and Correspondence of Vauvenargues* (2 vols., Paris: Furne, 1857), ii. 133.

without a single great battle, and it was considered a signal piece of good fortune when in the winter of 1742-43 Belle-Isle succeeded, with a loss of half his force, in leading by a long circuit, in the view of the enemy, and amid the horrors of famine and intense frost, some thirteen thousand men away from Prague. The King's Regiment took part in the Bohemian campaign, and in this frightful march that closed it; Vauvenargues with the rest.

To physical sufferings during two winters was added the distress of losing a comrade to whom he was devoted; he perished in the spring of 1742 under the hardships of the war. The *Éloge* in which Vauvenargues commemorates the virtues and the pitiful fate of his friend, is too deeply marked with the florid and declamatory style of youth to be pleasing to a more ripened taste.[1] He complained that nobody who had read it observed that it was touching, not remembering that even the most tender feeling fails to touch us when it has found stilted and turgid expression. Delicacy and warmth of affection were prominent characteristics in Vauvenargues. Perhaps if his life had been less severe, this fine susceptibility might have become fanciful and morbid. As it was, he loved his friends with a certain sweetness and equanimity in which there was never the faintest tinge of fretfulness, caprice, exacting vanity, or any of those other vices which betray in men the excessive consciousness of their

[1] *Éloge de P. H. de Seytres.* *Œuvres*, i. 141-150.

own personality which lies at the root of most of the obstacles in the way of an even and humane life. His nature had such depth and quality that the perpetual untowardness of circumstances left no evil print upon him; hardship made him not sour, but patient and wise, and there is no surer sign of generous temper.

The sufferings and bereavements of war were not his only trials. Vauvenargues was beset throughout the whole of his short life with the embarrassments of narrow means. His letters to Saint-Vincens, the most intimate of his friends, disclose the straits to which he was driven. The nature of these straits is an old story all over the world, and Vauvenargues did the same things that young men in want of money have generally done.

Vauvenargues has told us what he found the life of the camp. Luxurious and indolent living, neglected duties, discontented sighing after the delights of Paris, the exaltation of rank and mediocrity, an insolent contempt for merit; these were the characteristics of the men in high military place. The lower officers meantime were overwhelmed by an expenditure that the luxury of their superiors introduced and encouraged.[1]

To the considerations of an extravagant expenditure and the absence of every chance of promotion, there was added in the case of Vauvenargues the still more powerful drawback of irretrievably broken

[1] *Réflexions sur divers sujets*, i. 104.

health. The winter-march from Prague to Egra had sown fatal seed. His legs had been frost-bitten, and before they could be cured he was stricken by smallpox, which left him disfigured and almost blind. So after a service of nine years, he quitted military life (1744). He vainly solicited employment as a diplomatist. The career was not yet open to the talents, and in the memorial that Vauvenargues drew up he dwelt less on his conduct than on his birth, being careful to show that he had an authentic ancestor who was Governor of Hyères in the early part of the fourteenth century.[1] But the only road to employment lay through the court. The claims even of birth counted for nothing, unless they were backed by favour among the ignoble and unworthy fellow-creatures who haunted Versailles. For success it was essential to be not only high-born, but a parasite as well. 'Permit me to assure you, sir,' Vauvenargues wrote courageously to Amelot, then the minister, 'that it is this moral impossibility for a gentleman, with only zeal to commend him, of ever reaching the King his master, that causes the discouragement observed among the nobility of the provinces, that extinguishes all ambition.'[2] Amelot, to oblige Voltaire, eager as usual in good offices for his friend, answered the letters that Vauvenargues wrote, and promised to lay his name before the king as soon as a favourable opportunity should present itself.[3]

[1] *Œuvres*, ii. 249.   [2] *Ibid.* ii. 265.   [3] *Ibid.* ii. 266.

Vauvenargues was probably enough of a man of the world to take fair words of this sort at their value, and he had enough of qualities that do not belong to the man of the world to enable him to confront the disappointment with cheerful fortitude. 'Misfortune itself,' he had once written, 'has its charms in great extremities; for this opposition of fortune raises a courageous mind, and makes it collect all the forces that before were unemployed: it is in indolence and littleness that virtue suffers, when a timid prudence prevents it from rising in flight and forces it to creep along in bonds.'[1] He was true to the counsel he had thus given years before, and with the consciousness that death was fast approaching, and that all hope of advancement in the ordinary way was at an end, even if there were any chance of his life, he persevered in his project of going to Paris, there to earn the fame he instinctively felt that he had it in him to achieve. Neither scantiness of means nor the vehement protests of friends and relations—the worst foes to superior character on critical occasions—could detain him in the obscurity of Provence. In 1745 he took up his quarters in Paris in a humble house near the School of Medicine. Literature had not yet acquired the importance in France that it was so soon to obtain. The Encyclopædia was still unconceived, and the momentous work which that famous design was to accomplish, of organising the

[1] *Conseils à un jeune homme*, i. 124.

philosophers and men of letters into an army with banners, was still unexecuted. Voltaire, indeed, had risen, if not to the full height of his reputation, yet high enough both to command the admiration of people of quality, and to be the recognised chief of the new school of literature and thought. Voltaire had been struck by a letter in which Vauvenargues, then unknown to him, had sent a criticism comparing Corneille disadvantageously with Racine. Coming from a young officer, the member of a profession Voltaire frankly described as 'very noble, in truth, but slightly barbarous,' this criticism was peculiarly striking. A great many years afterwards Voltaire was surprised in the same way, to find that an officer could write such a book as the *Félicité publique* of the Marquis de Chastellux. To Vauvenargues he replied with many compliments, and pointed out with a good deal of pains the injustice the young critic had done to the great author of *Cinna*. '*It is the part of a man like you*,' he said admirably, '*to have preferences, but no exclusions.*'[1] The correspondence thus begun was kept up with ever-growing warmth and mutual respect. 'If you had been born a few years earlier,' Voltaire wrote to him, 'my works would be worth all the more for it; but at any rate, even at the close of my career, you confirm me in the path you pursue.'[2]

The personal impression was as fascinating as that which had been conveyed by Vauvenargues'

[1] *Œuvres*, ii. 252.   [2] *Ibid.* ii. 272.

letters. Voltaire took every opportunity of visiting his unfortunate friend, then each day drawing nearer to the grave. Men of humbler stature were equally attracted. 'It was at this time,' says the light-hearted Marmontel, 'that I first saw at home the man who had a charm for me beyond all the rest of the world, the good, the virtuous, the wise Vauvenargues. Cruelly used by nature in his body, he was in soul one of her rarest masterpieces. I seemed to see in him Fénelon weak and suffering. I could make a good book of his conversations, if I had had a chance of collecting them. You see some traces of it in the selection that he has left of his thoughts and meditations. But all eloquent and full of feeling as he is in his writings, he was still more so in his conversation.'[1] Marmontel felt sincere grief when Vauvenargues died, and in the *Epistle to Voltaire* expressed his sorrow in some fair lines. They contain the happy phrase applied to Vauvenargues, '*ce cœur stoïque et tendre.*'[2]

In religious sentiment Vauvenargues was out of the groove of his time. That is to say here he was not unsusceptible. Accepting no dogma, so far as we can judge, and complying with no observances, very faint and doubtful as to even the fundamentals, he never partook of the furious and bitter antipathy

[1] *Mémoires de Marmontel*, vol. i. 189.

[2] The reader of Marmontel's *Mémoires* will remember the extraordinary and grotesque circumstances under which a younger brother of Mirabeau (of *l'ami des hommes*, that is) appealed to the memory of Vauvenargues. See vol. i. 256-260.

of the first men of that century against the Church, its creeds, and its book. At one time, as will be seen from a passage to be quoted by and by, his leanings were towards that vague and indefinable doctrine which identifies God with all the forces and their manifestations in the universe. Afterwards even this adumbration of a theistic explanation of the world seems to have passed from him, and he lived, as many other men, not bad, have lived, with the fair working substitute for a religious doctrine that is provided in the tranquil search, or the acceptance in a devotional spirit, of all larger mortal experiences and higher human impressions. There is a *Meditation on the Faith*, including a *Prayer*, among his writings; and there can be little doubt, in spite of Condorcet's incredible account of the circumstances of its composition, that it is the expression of what was at the time a sincere feeling.[1] It is, however, rather the straining and ecstatic rhapsody of one who ardently seeks faith, than the calm and devout assurance of him who already possesses it. Vauvenargues was religious by temperament, but he could not entirely resist the intellectual influences of the period. The one fact delivered him from dogma and superstition, and the other from scoffing and harsh unspirituality. He saw that apart from the question of the truth or falsehood of its historic basis, there was a balance to be struck between the consolations and the

[1] *Œuvres*, i. 225-232.

afflictions of the faith.[1] Practically he was content to leave this balance unstruck, and to pass by on the other side. Scarcely any of his maxims concern religion. One of these few is worth quoting, where he says: 'The strength or weakness of our belief depends more on our courage than our light; not all those who mock at auguries have more intellect than those who believe in them.'[2]

The end came in the spring of 1747, when Vauvenargues was no more than thirty-two. Perhaps, in spite of his physical miseries, these two years in Paris were the least unhappy time in his life. He was in the great centre where the fame he longed for was earned and liberally awarded. A year of intercourse with so full and alert and brilliant a mind as Voltaire's must have been more to one so appreciative of mental greatness as Vauvenargues, than many years of intercourse with subalterns in the Regiment of the King. With death, now known to be very near at hand, he had made his account before. 'To execute great things,' he had written in a maxim which gained the lively praise of Voltaire, 'a man must live as though he had never to die.'[3] This mood was common among the Greeks and Romans;

---

[1] *Letter to Saint-Vincens*, ii. 46.   [2] No. 318.

[3] Napoleon said on some occasion, '*Il faut vouloir vivre et savoir mourir.*' M. Littré prefaces the third volume of that heroic monument of learning and industry, his *Dictionary of the French Language,* by the words: 'He who wishes to employ his life seriously ought always to act as if he had long to live, and to govern himself as if he would have soon to die.'

but the religion which Europe accepted later retained the mark of its dismal origin nowhere so strongly as in the distorted prominence it gave in the minds of its votaries to the dissolution of the body. It was one of the first conditions of the Revival of Reason that the dreary *memento mori* and its emblems should be deliberately effaced. 'The thought of death,' said Vauvenargues, 'leads us astray, because it makes us forget to live.' He did not understand living in the dissolute sense. The libertinism of his regiment called no severe rebuke from him, but his meditative temper drew him away from it even in his youth. It is not impossible that if his days had not been cut short, he might have impressed Parisian society with ideas and a sentiment that would have left to it all its cheerfulness, and yet prevented the laxity that so fatally weakened it. Turgot, the only other conspicuous man who could have withstood the licence of the time, had probably too much of the austerity that is in the fibre of so many great characters, to make any moral counsels he might have given widely effective.

Vauvenargues was sufficiently free from all taint of the pedagogue or the preacher to have dispelled the sophisms of licence, less by argument than by the attraction of virtue in his own character. The stock moralist fails to touch the hearts of men, or to affect their lives, for lack of delicacy, of sympathy, and of freshness; he attempts to compensate for this by excess of emphasis, and that more often repels than persuades us. Vauvenargues, on the other hand, is remarkable for delicacy and half-reserved tenderness. Everything that he has said is coloured and warmed with feeling for the infirmities of men. He writes not merely as an analytical outsider. Hence, unlike most moralists, he is no satirist. He had borne the burdens. 'The looker-on,' runs one of his maxims, 'softly lying in a carpeted chamber, inveighs against the soldier, who passes winter nights on the river's edge, and keeps watch in silence over the safety of the land.'[1] Vauvenargues had been something very different from the safe and sheltered critic of other men's battles, and this is the secret of the hold that his words have. They are real, with the reality that can only come from two sources: from high poetic imagination, which Vauvenargues did not possess, or else from experience of life acting on and strengthening a generous nature. 'The cause of most books of morality being so insipid,' he says, 'is, that their authors are not sincere; that, being feeble echoes of one another, they could not venture to publish their own real maxims and private sentiments.'[2] One of the secrets of his own freedom from this ordinary insipidity of moralists was his freedom also from their oracular pretence.

Besides these positive merits, he had, as we have said, the negative distinction of never being emphatic; his sayings are nearly always moderate and persuasive,

[1] No. 223. [2] No. 300.

alike in sentiment and in phrase. Sometimes they are almost tentative in the diffidence of their turn. Compared with him La Rochefoucauld's is hard, and La Bruyère's sententious. In the moralist who aspires to move and win men by their best side instead of their worst, the absence of this hardness and the presence of a certain lambency and play even in the exposition of truths of perfect assurance, are essential conditions of psychagogic quality. In religion such law does not hold, and the contagion of fanaticism is most rapidly spread by a rigorous and cheerless example.

We may notice in passing that Vauvenargues has the defects of his qualities, and that with his aversion to emphasis was bound up a certain inability to appreciate even grandeur and originality, if they were too strongly and boldly marked. 'It is easy to criticise an author,' he has said, 'but hard to estimate him.'[1] This was never more unfortunately proved than in the remarks of Vauvenargues himself upon Molière. It is hard to forgive a writer who can say that 'La Bruyère, animated with nearly the same genius, painted the crookedness of men with as much truth and as much force as Molière; but I believe that there is more eloquence and more elevation to be found in La Bruyère's images.'[2] Without at all undervaluing La Bruyère, one of the acutest and finest of writers, we may say that this is a disas-

---

[1] No. 264.
[2] *Réflexions critiques sur quelques poètes*, i. 237.

trous piece of criticism. Quite as unhappy is the preference given to Racine over Molière, not merely for the conclusion arrived at, but for the reasons on which it is founded. Molière's subjects, we read, are low, his language negligent and incorrect, his characters bizarre and eccentric. Racine, on the other hand, takes sublime themes, presents us with noble types, and writes with simplicity and elegance. It is not enough to concede to Racine the glory of art, while giving to Molière or Corneille the glory of genius. 'When people speak of the art of Racine—the art that puts things in their place; characterises men, their passions, manners, genius; banishes obscurities, superfluities, false brilliancies; paints nature with fire, sublimity, and grace—what can we think of such art as this, except that it is the genius of extraordinary men, and the origin of those rules that writers without genius embrace with so much zeal and so little success?'[1] And it is certainly true that the art of Racine implied genius. The defect of the criticism lies, as usual, in a failure to see that there is glory enough in both; in the art of highly finished composition and presentation, and in the art of bold and striking creation. Yet Vauvenargues was able to discern the secret of the popularity of Molière, and the foundation of the common opinion that no other dramatist had carried his own kind of art so far as Molière had carried his; 'the reason is, I fancy, that he is more natural than any of the others, and

[1] Œuvres, i. 248.

this is an important lesson for everybody who wishes to write.'[1] He did not see how nearly everything went in this concession that Molière was, above all, natural. With equal truth of perception he condemned the affectation of grandeur lent by the French tragedians to classical personages who were in truth simple and natural, as the principal defect of the national drama, and the common rock on which their poets made shipwreck.[2] Let us, however, rejoice for the sake of the critical reputation of Vauvenargues that he was unable to read Shakespeare. One for whom Molière is too eccentric, grotesque, inelegant, was not likely to do much justice to the mightiest but most irregular of all dramatists.

A man's prepossessions in dramatic poetry, supposing him to be cultivated enough to have any, furnish the most certain clue that we can get to the spirit in which he inwardly regards character and conduct. The uniform and reasoned preference that Vauvenargues had for Racine over Molière and Corneille, was only the transfer to art of the balanced, moderate, normal, and harmonious temper he brought to the survey of human nature. Excess was a condition of thought, feeling, and speech, in every form disagreeable to him; alike in the gloom of Pascal's reveries, and in the inflation of speech of some of the heroes of Corneille. He failed to relish even Montaigne as he ought to have done, because Montaigne's method was

[1] *Réflexions critiques sur quelques poètes*, i. 238.
[2] *Œuvres*, i. 243.

too prolix, his scepticism too universal, his egoism too manifest, and because he did not produce complete and artistic wholes.[1]

Reasonableness is the strongest mark in Vauvenargues' thinking; balance, evenness, purity of vision, penetration finely toned with indulgence. He is never betrayed into criticism of men from the point of view of immutable first principles. Perhaps this was what the elder Mirabeau meant when he wrote to Vauvenargues, who was his cousin: 'You have the English genius to perfection,' and what Vauvenargues meant when he wrote of himself to Mirabeau: 'Nobody in the world has a mind less French than I.'[2] These international comparisons are among the least fruitful of literary amusements, even when they happen not to be extremely misleading; as when, for example, Voltaire called Locke the English Pascal, a description that can only be true on condition that the qualifying adjective is meant to strip either Locke or Pascal of most of his characteristic traits. And if we compare Vauvenargues with any of our English aphoristic writers, there is not resemblance enough to make the contrast instructive. The obvious truth is that in this department our literature is weak, while French literature is particularly strong. With the exception of Bacon, we have no writer of apophthegms of the first order; and the difference between Bacon as a moralist and Pascal or Vauvenargues, is the difference between Polonius's famous

[1] *Œuvres*, i. 275.   [2] *Correspondance. Ibid.* ii. 131, 207.

discourse to Laertes and the soliloquy of Hamlet. Bacon's precepts refer rather to external conduct and worldly fortune than to the inner composition of character, or to the 'wide, grey, lampless' depths of human destiny. We find the same national characteristic, though on an infinitely lower level, in Franklin's oracular saws. Among the French sages a psychological element is predominant, as well as an occasional transcendent loftiness of feeling, not to be found in Bacon's wisest maxims, and from his point of view in their composition we could not expect to find them there. We seek in vain amid the positivity of Bacon, or the quaint and timorous paradox of Browne, or the acute sobriety of Shaftesbury, for any of the poetic pensiveness that is strong in Vauvenargues, and reaches tragic heights in Pascal.[1] Addison may have the delicacy of Vauvenargues, but it is a delicacy that wants the stir and warmth of feeling. It seems as if with English writers poetic sentiment naturally sought expression in poetic forms, while the Frenchmen of nearly corresponding temperament were restrained within the limits of prose by reason of the rigorously prescribed stateliness and stiffness of their verse at that time. A man in this country with the quality of Vauvenargues,

[1] Long-winded and tortuous and difficult to seize as Shaftesbury is as a whole, in detached sentences he shows marked aphoristic quality; *e.g.* 'The most ingenious way of becoming foolish is by a system'; 'The liker anything is to wisdom, if it be not plainly the thing itself, the more directly it becomes its opposite.'

with his delicacy, tenderness, elevation, would have composed lyrics. We have undoubtedly lost much by the laxity and irregularity of our verse, but as undoubtedly we owe to its freedom some of the most perfect and delightful of the minor figures that adorn the noble gallery of English poets.

It would be an error to explain the superiority of the great French moralists by supposing in them a fancy and imagination too defective for poetic art. It was the circumstances of the national literature during the seventeenth and eighteenth centuries that made Vauvenargues, for instance, a composer of aphorisms, rather than a moral poet like Pope. Let us remember some of his own most discriminating words. 'Who has more imagination,' he asks, ' than Bossuet, Montaigne, Descartes, Pascal, all of them great philosophers? Who more judgment and wisdom than Racine, Boileau, La Fontaine, Molière, all of them poets full of genius? *It is not true, then, that the ruling qualities exclude the others; on the contrary, they suppose them.* I should be much surprised if a great poet were without vivid lights on philosophy, at any rate moral philosophy, and it will very seldom happen for a true philosopher to be totally devoid of imagination.'[1] With imagination in the highest sense Vauvenargues was not largely endowed, but he had as much as is essential to reveal to one that the hard and sober-judging faculty is not the single, nor even the main element, in a wise and full intelligence.

[1] No. 278 (i. 411).

'All my philosophy,' he wrote to Mirabeau, when only four- or five-and-twenty years old, an age when the intellect is usually most exigent of supremacy, 'all my philosophy has its source in my heart.'[1]

In the same spirit he had well said that there is more cleverness in the world than greatness of soul, more people with talent than with lofty character.[2] Hence some of the most peculiarly characteristic and impressive of his aphorisms; that famous one, for instance, '*Great thoughts come from the heart*,' and the rest which hang upon the same idea. 'Virtuous instinct has no need of reason, but supplies it.' 'Reason misleads us more often than nature.' 'Reason does not know the interests of the heart.' 'Perhaps we owe to the passions the greatest advantages of the intellect.' Such sayings are only true on condition that instinct and nature and passion have been already moulded under the influence of reason; just as this other saying, which won the admiration of Voltaire, '*Magnanimity owes no account of its motives to prudence*,' is only true on condition that by magnanimity we understand a mood not out of accord with the loftiest kind of prudence.[3] But in the eighteenth century reason

[1] *Œuvres*, ii. 115.
[2] *Ibid*. i. 87.

[3] Doch
Zuweilen ist des Sinns in einer Sache
Auch mehr, als wir vermuthen; und es wäre
So unerhört doch nicht, dass uns der Heiland

and prudence were words current in their lower and narrower sense, and thus one coming like Vauvenargues to see this lowness and narrowness, sought to invest ideas and terms that in fact only involved modifications of these with a significance of direct antagonism. Magnanimity was contrasted inimically with prudence, and instinct and nature were made to thrust from their throne reason and reflection. Carried to its limit, this tendency developed the speculative and social excesses of the great sentimental school. In Vauvenargues it was only the moderate, just, and most seasonable protest of a fine observer, against the supremacy among ideals of a narrow, deliberative, and calculating spirit.

His exaltation of virtuous instinct over reason is in a curious way parallel to Burke's memorable exaltation over reason of prejudice. 'Prejudice,' said Burke, 'previously engages the mind in a steady course of wisdom and virtue, and does not leave the man hesitating in the moment of decision, sceptical, puzzled, and unresolved. Prejudice renders a man's virtue his habit, and not a series of unconnected acts;

Auf Wegen zu sich zöge, die der Kluge
Von selbst nicht leicht betreten würde.
Nathan der Weise, iii. 10.
But
Sometimes there is more purpose in a cause
Than we may have conjectured; and it were
Not quite unheard-of if the Saviour drew
Us to him by such paths as world-wise men
Would hesitate to take of their own choice.

through just prejudice his duty becomes a part of his nature.'[1] What Burke designated as prejudice, Vauvenargues less philosophically styled virtuous instinct; each meant precisely the same thing, though the difference of phrase implied a different view of its origin and growth; and the side opposite to each of them was the same—namely, a sophisticated and over-refining intelligence, narrowed to the consideration of particular circumstances as they presented themselves.

Translated into the modern equivalent, the heart, nature, instinct of Vauvenargues all mean *character*. He insisted upon spontaneous impulse as a condition of all greatest thought and action. Men think and work on the highest level when they move without conscious and deliberate strain after virtue : when, in other words, their habitual motives, aims, methods, their character, in short, naturally draw them into the region of what is virtuous. *'It is by our ideas that we ennoble our passions or we debase them ; they rise high or sink low according to the man's soul.'*[2] All this has ceased to be new to our generation, but when Vauvenargues was writing, and indeed in days much nearer to us than that, the key to all nobleness was thought to be found only by cool balancing and prudential calculation. A book like *Clarissa Harlowe* shows us this prudential and calculating temper

---

[1] *Reflections on the French Revolution. Works* (ed. 1842), i. 414.
[2] *Œuvres*, ii. 170.

underneath a varnish of sentimentalism and fine feelings, an incongruous and extremely displeasing combination, particularly characteristic of certain sets and circles in that century. One of the distinctions of Vauvenargues is that exaltation of sentiment did not with him cloak a substantial adherence to a low prudence, nor to the fragment of reason that has so constantly usurped the name and place of the whole. He eschewed the too common compromise the sentimentalist makes with reflection and calculation, and this saved him from being a sentimentalist.

The doctrine of the predominance of the heart over the head, that has brought forth so many pernicious and destructive fantasies in the history of social thought, represented in his case no more than a reaction against the great detractors of humanity. Rochefoucauld had surveyed mankind exclusively from the point of their vain and egoistic propensities, and his aphorisms are profoundly true of all persons in whom these propensities are habitually supreme, and of all the world in so far as these propensities happen to influence them. Pascal, on the one hand, leaving the affections and inclinations of a man very much on one side, had directed all his efforts to showing the pitiful feebleness and incurable helplessness of man in the sphere of the understanding. Vauvenargues is thus confronted by two sinister pictures of humanity—the one of its moral meanness and littleness, the other of its intellectual poverty and impotency. He turned away from both of them, and found in magnanimous and unsophisticated feeling, of which he was conscious in himself and observant in others, a compensation alike for the selfishness of some men and the intellectual limitations of all men. This compensation was ample enough to restore the human self-respect that Pascal and Rochefoucauld had done their best to weaken.

The truth in that disparagement was indisputable so far as it went. It was not a kind of truth, however, on which it is good for the world much to dwell, and it is the thinkers like Vauvenargues who build up and inspire high resolve. 'Scarcely any maxim,' runs one of his own, 'is true in all respects.'[1] We must take them in pairs to find out the mean truth; and to understand the ways of men, so far as words about men can help us, we must read with appreciation not only Vauvenargues, who said that great thoughts come from the heart, but La Rochefoucauld, who called the intelligence the dupe of the heart, and Pascal, who saw only desperate creatures, miserably perishing before one another's eyes in the grim dungeon of the universe. Yet it is the observer in the spirit of Vauvenargues, of whom we must always say that he has chosen the better part. Vauvenargues' own estimate was sound. 'The Duke of La Rochefoucauld seized to perfection the weak side of human nature; maybe he knew its strength too; and only contested the merit of so many splendid actions in

[1] No. 111.

order to unmask false wisdom. Whatever his design, the effect seems to me mischievous; his book, filled with delicate invective against hypocrisy, even to this day turns men away from virtue, by persuading them that it is never genuine.'[1] Or, as he put it elsewhere, without express personal reference: 'You must arouse in men the feeling of their prudence and strength, if you would raise their character; those who only apply themselves to bring out the absurdities and weaknesses of mankind, enlighten the judgment of the public far less than they deprave its inclination.'[2] This principle was implied in Goethe's excellent saying, that if you would improve a man, it is best to begin by persuading him that he is already that which you would have him to be.

To talk in this way was to bring men out from the pits that cynicism on the one side, and asceticism on the other, had dug so deep for them, back to the warm precincts of the cheerful day. The cynic and the ascetic had each looked at life through a microscope, exaggerating blemishes, distorting proportions, filling the eye with ugly and repulsive illusions.[3] Humanity, as was said, was in disgrace with the

[1] *Œuvres*, ii. 74.
[2] No. 285.
[3] 'A man may as well pretend to cure himself of love by viewing his mistress through the artificial medium of a microscope or prospect, and beholding there the coarseness of her skin and monstrous disproportion of her features, as hope to excite or moderate any passion by the artificial arguments of a Seneca or an Epictetus.'—Hume's *Essays* (xviii. *The Sceptic*).

thinkers. The maxims of Vauvenargues were a plea for a return to a healthy and normal sense of relations. 'These philosophers,' he cried, 'are men, yet they do not speak in human language; they change all the ideas of things, and misuse all their terms.'[1] These are some of the most direct of his retorts upon Pascal and La Rochefoucauld:

'I have always felt it to be absurd for philosophers to fabricate a Virtue that is incompatible with the nature of humanity, and then after having pretended this, to declare coldly that there is no virtue. If they are speaking of the phantom of their imagination, they may of course abandon or destroy it as they please, for they invented it; but true virtue—which they cannot be brought to call by this name, because it is not in conformity with their definitions; which is the work of nature and not their own; and which consists mainly in goodness and vigour of soul—that does not depend on their fancies, and will last for ever with characters that cannot possibly be effaced.'

'The body has its graces, the intellect its talents; is the heart then to have nothing but vices? And must man, who is capable of reason, be incapable of virtue?'

'We are susceptible of friendship, justice, humanity, compassion, and reason. O my friends, what then is virtue?'

'Disgust is no mark of health, nor is appetite

[1] *Œuvres*, i. 163.

a disorder; quite the reverse. Thus we think of the body, but we judge the soul on other principles. We suppose that a strong soul is one that is exempt from passions, and as youth is more active and ardent than later age, we look on it as a time of fever, and place the strength of man in his decay.'[1]

The theological speculator insists that virtue lies in a constant and fierce struggle between the will and the passions, between man and human nature. Vauvenargues founded his whole theory of life on the doctrine that the will is not something independent of passions, inclinations, and ideas, but on the contrary is an index moved and fixed by them, as the hand of a clock follows the operation of the mechanical forces within. Character is an integral unit. 'Whether it is reason or passion that moves us, it is we who determine ourselves; it would be madness to distinguish one's thoughts and sentiments from one's self. . . . No will in men, which does not owe its direction to their temperament, their reasoning, and their actual feelings.'[2] Virtue, then, is not necessarily a condition of strife between the will and the rest of our faculties and passions; no such strife is possible, for the will obeys the preponderant passion or idea, or group of passions and ideas; and the contest lies between one passion, or group, and another. Hence, in right character there is no

[1] Nos. 296-298, 148.
[2] *Sur le Libre Arbitre.* Œuvres, i. 199.

struggle at all, for the virtuous inclinations naturally and easily direct our will and actions; virtue is then independent of struggle; and the circumstance of our finding pleasure in this and the practice, is no reason why the practice or that pleasure should not be virtuous beyond impeachment.

It is easy to see the connection between this theory of the dependence of the will, and the prominence Vauvenargues is ever giving to the passions. These are the key to the movements of the will. To direct and shape the latter, you must educate the former. It was for his perception of this truth, we may notice in passing, that Comte awarded to Vauvenargues a place in the Positivist Calendar; 'for his direct effort, in spite of the universal desuetude into which it had fallen, to reorganise the culture of the heart according to a better knowledge of human nature, of which this noble thinker discerned the centre to be affective.'[1]

Vauvenargues showed his genuine healthiness not more by a plenary rejection of the doctrine of the incurable vileness and frenzy of man, than by his freedom from the boisterous transcendental optimism which has too many votaries in our time. He would not have men told that they are miserable earth-gnomes, the slaves of a black destiny, but he still placed them a good deal lower than the angels. For instance: 'We are too inattentive or too much occupied with ourselves, to get to the bottom of one

[1] *Politique positive*, iii. 589.

another's characters; *whoever has watched masks at a ball dancing together in a friendly manner, and joining hands without knowing who the others are, and then parting the moment afterwards never to meet again nor ever to regret, or be regretted, can form some idea of the world.*'[1] But then, as he said elsewhere: ' We can be perfectly aware of our imperfection, without being humiliated by the sight. *One of the noblest qualities of our nature is that we are able so easily to dispense with greater perfection.*'[2] In all this we mark the large and rational humaneness of the new time, a tolerant and kindly and elevating estimate of men.

The faith in the natural and simple operation of virtue, without the aid of all sorts of valetudinarian restrictions, comes out on every occasion. The Trappist theory of the conditions of virtue found no quarter with him. Mirabeau, for instance, complained of the atmosphere of the court, as fatal to the practice of virtue. Vauvenargues replied that the people there were doubtless no better than they should be, and that vice was dominant. ' So much the worse for those who have vices. But when you are fortunate enough to possess virtue, it is, to my thinking, a very noble ambition to lift up this same virtue in the bosom of corruption, to make it succeed, to place it above all, to indulge and control the passions without reproach, to overthrow the obstacles to them, and to surrender yourself to the inclinations of an upright

[1] No. 330. [2] Nos. 462, 463.

and magnanimous heart, instead of combating or concealing them in retreat, without either satisfying or vanquishing them. I know nothing so weak and so vain as to flee before vices, or to hate them without measure; for people only hate them by way of reprisal because they are afraid of them, or else out of vengeance because these vices have played them some sorry turn; but a little loftiness of soul, some knowledge of the heart, a gentle and tranquil humour, will protect you against the risk of being either surprised, or keenly wounded by them.'[1]

His *Characters*, very little known in this country, are as excellent as any work in this kind that we are acquainted with, or probably as excellent as such work can be. They are real and natural, yet while abstaining as rigorously as Vauvenargues everywhere does from grotesque and extravagant traits, they avoid equally the vice of presenting the mere bald and sterile flats of character, which he that runs may read. As we have said, he had the quality possessed by so few of those who write about men; he watched men, and drew from the life. In a word, he studied concrete examples and interrogated his own experience—the only sure guarantee that one writing on his themes has anything which it is worth our while to listen to. Among other consequences of this reality of their source is the agreeable fact that these pictures are free from that clever bitterness and easy sarcasm, by which crude and jejune observers,

[1] *Correspondance. Œuvres*, ii. 163.

thinking more of their own wit than of what they observe, sometimes gain reputation. Even the coxcombs, self-duping knaves, simpletons, braggarts, and other evil types whom he selects, are drawn with unstrained and simple conformity to reality. The pictures have no moral label pinned on to them. Yet Vauvenargues took life seriously enough, and it was just because he took it seriously, that he had no inclination to air his wit or practise a verbal humour upon the stuff out of which happiness and misery are made.

One or two fragments will suffice. Take the Man of the World:

'A man of the world is not he who knows other men best, who has most foresight or dexterity in affairs, who is most instructed by experience and study; he is neither a good manager, nor a man of science, nor a politician, nor a skilful officer, nor a painstaking magistrate. He is a man who is ignorant of nothing but who knows nothing; who, doing his own business ill, fancies himself very capable of doing that of other people; a man who has much useless wit, who has the art of saying flattering things which do not flatter, and judicious things which give no information; who can persuade nobody, though he speaks well; endowed with that sort of eloquence which can bring out trifles, and which annihilates great subjects; as penetrating in what is ridiculous and external in men, as he is blind to the depths of their minds. One who, afraid of being wearisome by reason, is wearisome by his extravagances; is jocose without gaiety, and lively without passion.'[1]

Or the following, the Inconstant Man:

'Such a man seems really to possess more than one character. A powerful imagination makes his soul take the shape of all the objects that affect it; he suddenly astonishes the world by acts of generosity and courage which were never expected of him; the image of virtue inflames, elevates, softens, masters his heart; he receives the impression from the loftiest, and he surpasses them. But when his imagination has grown cold, his courage droops, his generosity sinks; the vices opposed to these virtues take possession of his soul, and after having reigned awhile supreme, they make way for other objects. . . . We cannot say that they have a great nature, or strong, or weak, or light; it is a swift and imperious imagination that reigns with sovereign power over all their being, subjugates their genius, and prescribes for them in turn those fine actions and those faults, those heights and those littlenesses, those flights of enthusiasm and those fits of disgust, which we are wrong in charging either with hypocrisy or madness.'[2]

Let us note that Vauvenargues is almost entirely free from the favourite trick of the aphoristic person, that consists in forming a series of sentences, the predicates being various qualifications of extravagance, vanity, and folly, and the subject being Women. On the one or two occasions in which he

[1] *Œuvres*, i. 310. [2] *Ibid.* i. 325.

begins the maxim with the fatal words, *Les femmes*, he is as little profound as other people who persist in thinking of man and woman as two different species. 'Women,' for example, 'have ordinarily more vanity than temperament, and more temperament than virtue'—which is fairly true of all human beings, and in so far as it is true, describes men just as exactly —and no more so—as it describes women. In truth, Vauvenargues felt too seriously about conduct and character to go far in this direction. Now and again he is content with a mere smartness, as when he says: 'There are some thoroughly excellent people who cannot get rid of their *ennui* except at the expense of society.' But such a mood is not common. He is usually grave, and not seldom profoundly weighty, delicate without being weak, and subtle without obscurity; as for example:

'People teach children to fear and obey; the avarice, pride, or timidity of the fathers, instructs the children in economy, arrogance, or submission. We stir them up to be yet more and more copyists, which they are only too disposed to be, as it is; nobody thinks of making them original, hardy, independent.'

'If instead of dulling the vivacity of children, people did their best to raise the impulsiveness and movement of their characters, what might we not expect from a fine natural temper?'

Again: 'The moderation of the weak is mediocrity.'

'What is arrogance in the weak is elevation in the strong; as the strength of a sick man is frenzy, and that of a whole man is vigour.'

'It is a great sign of mediocrity always to praise moderately.'

Vauvenargues has a saying to the effect that men very often, without thinking of it, form an idea of their face and expression from the ruling sentiment of which they are conscious in themselves at the time. He hints that this is perhaps the reason why a coxcomb always believes himself to be handsome.[1] And in a letter to Mirabeau, he describes pleasantly how sometimes in moments of distraction he pictures himself with an air of loftiness, of majesty, of penetration, according to the idea that is occupying his mind, and how if by chance he sees his face in the mirror, he is nearly as much amazed as if he saw a Cyclops or a Tartar.[2] Yet his nature, if we may trust the portrait, revealed itself in his face; it is one of the most attractive to look upon, even in the cold inarticulateness of an engraving. We may read his character in the soft strength of the brow, the meditative lines of mouth and chin, above all, the striking clearness, the self-collection, the feminine solicitude, that mingle freely and without eagerness or expectancy in his gaze, as though he were hearkening to some everflowing inward stream of divine melody. We think of the gracious touch in Bacon's picture of the father

[1] No. 236.   [2] *Œuvres*, ii. 188.

of Solomon's House, that 'he had an aspect as though he pitied men.' If we reproach France in the eighteenth century with its coarseness, artificiality, shallowness, because it produced such men as Duclos, we ought to remember that this was also the century of Vauvenargues, one of the most tender, lofty, cheerful, and delicately sober of all the company of moralists.

A FEW WORDS ON FRENCH MODELS.[1]

> Nunquamne reponam,
> Vexatus toties rauci Theseide Codri?

THE French Revolution has furnished the enemies of each successive proposal of reform with a boundless supply of prejudicial analogies, appalling parallels, and ugly nicknames, that are all just as conclusive with the unwise as if they were the aptest of arguments. Sydney Smith might well put 'the awful example of a neighbouring nation' among the standing topics of the Noodle's Oration. The abolition of rotten boroughs brought down a thousand ominous references to noyades, fusillades, and guillotines. When Sir Robert Peel took the duty off corn, Croker warned him with due solemnity that he was breaking up the old interests, dividing the great families, and beginning exactly such a catastrophe as did the Noailles and the Montmorencis in 1789. Cobden and Bright were promiscuously likened to Babœuf, Chaumette, and Anacharsis Clootz. Babœuf, it is true, was for dividing up all property, and Chaumette

[1] March 1888.

was an aggressive atheist; but these were mere *nuances*, not material to the purposes of obloquy. Robespierre, Danton, Marat have been mercilessly trotted forth in their sanguinary shrouds, and treated as the counterparts and precursors of worthies so obviously and exactly like them as Mr. Beales and Mr. Odger; while an innocent caucus for the registration of voters recalls to some well-known writers lurid visions of the Cordeliers and the Jacobin Club.

A recent addition has been made to the stock of nicknames drawn from the terrible melodrama of the eighteenth century. The Chancellor of the Exchequer, afterwards Lord Goschen, at Dublin, described the present very humble writer as 'the Saint-Just of our Revolution.' The description was received with lively applause. It would be indelicate to wonder how many in a hundred, even in that audience of the elect, had ever heard of Saint-Just, how many in five hundred could have spelt his name, and how many in a thousand could have told any three facts in his career. But let us muse for a moment upon the portrait. I take down the first picture of Saint-Just that comes to my hand. M. Taine is the artist:

'Among these energetic nullities we see gradually rising a young monster—with face handsome and tranquil—Saint-Just! A sort of precocious Sulla, who at five-and-twenty suddenly springs from the ranks, and by force of atrocity wins his place! Six years before, he began life by an act of domestic robbery: while on a visit at his mother's, he ran away in the night with her plate and jewels; for that he was locked up for six months. On his release, he employed his leisure in the composition of an odious poem. Then he flung himself head foremost into the Revolution. Blood calcined by study, a colossal pride, a conscience completely unhinged, an imagination haunted by the bloody recollections of Rome and Sparta, an intelligence falsified and twisted until it found itself most at its ease in the practice of enormous paradox, barefaced sophism, and murderous lying— all these perilous ingredients, mixed in a furnace of concentrated ambition, boiled and fermented long and silently in his breast.'

One may entertain demons unawares, and have calcined blood without being a bit the wiser. Still, we do not find the likeness striking. It would have done just as well to be called Nero, Torquemada, Iago, or Bluebeard. Whether the present writer does or does not deserve all the compliments that history has paid to Saint-Just, is a very slight and trivial question, with which the public will naturally not much concern itself. But as some use is from time to time made of the writer's imputed delinquencies to prejudice an important cause, it is perhaps worth while to try in a page or two to give a better account of things. It is true that he has written on revolutionists like Robespierre, and on destructive thinkers like Rousseau and Voltaire. It is true that he believes the two latter to have been on the whole, when all deductions are made, on the side of human progress. But what sort of foundation is this for the inference that he 'finds his models in the heroes of the French Revolution,' and 'looks for his methods in the Reign of Terror'? It would be equally logical to infer that because I have written, not without sympathy and appreciation, of Joseph de Maistre, I therefore find my model in a hero of the Catholic Reaction, and look for my methods in the revived supremacy of the Holy See over all secular and temporal authorities. It would be just as fair to say that because I pointed out, as it was the critic's business to do, the many admirable merits, and the important moral influences on the society of that time, of the *New Heloïsa*, therefore I am bound to think Saint-Preux a very fine fellow, particularly fit to be a model and a hero for young Ireland. Only on the principle that who drives fat oxen must himself be fat, can it be held that who writes on Danton must be himself in all circumstances a Dantonist.

The most insignificant of literary contributions have a history and an origin; and the history of these contributions is short and simple enough. Carlyle with all the force of his humoristic genius had impressed upon his generation an essentially one-sided view both of the eighteenth century as a whole, and of the French thinkers of that century in particular. His essay on Diderot, his lecture on Rousseau, his chapters on Voltaire, with all their brilliance, penetration, and incomparable satire, were the high-water mark in this country of the literary reaction against the French school of Revolution. Everybody knows the famous diatribes against the Bankrupt Century and all its men and all its works. Voltaire's furies, Diderot's indigestions, Rousseau's amours, and the odd tricks and shifts of the whole of them and their company, offered ready material for the boisterous horseplay of the transcendental humorist. Then the tide began to turn. Buckle's book on the history of civilisation had something to do with it. But it was the historical chapters in Comte's *Positive Philosophy* that first opened the minds of many of us, who, these many years ago, were young men, to a very different judgment of the true place of those schools in the literary and social history of western Europe. We learnt to perceive that though much in the thought and the lives of the literary precursors of the Revolution laid them fairly open to Carlyle's banter, yet banter was not all, and even grave condemnation was not all. In essays, like mine, written from this point of view, and with the object of trying to trim the balance rather more correctly, it may well have been that the better side of the thinkers concerned was sometimes unduly dwelt upon, and their worse side unduly left in the background. It may well have been that an impression of personal adhesion was conveyed that only very partially existed, or even where it did not exist at all : that is a risk of misinterpretation which it is always hard for the historical critic to escape. There may have been a too eager tone ; but to be eager is not a very bad vice at any age under the critical forty. There were some needlessly aggressive passages, and some sallies that ought to have been avoided, because they gave pain to good people. There was perhaps too much of the particular excitement of the time. It was the date when *Essays and Reviews* was still thought a terrible explosive; when Bishop Colenso's arithmetical tests as to the flocks and herds of the children of Israel were believed to be sapping not only the inspiration of the Pentateuch but the foundations of the Faith and the Church; and when Darwin's scientific speculations were shaking the civilised world. Some excitement was to be pardoned in days like those, and I am quite sure that one side needed pardon at least as much as the other. For the substantial soundness of the general views I took of the French revolutionary thinkers at that time, I feel no apprehension; nor—some possible occasional phrases or sentences excepted and apart—do I see the smallest reason to shrink or to depart from any one of them. So far as one particular reference may serve to illustrate the tenour of the whole body of criticism, the following lines, which close my chapter on the Encyclopædia, will answer the purpose as well as any others, and I shall perhaps be excused for transcribing them:

'An urgent social task lay before France and before Europe: it could not be postponed until the thinkers had worked out a scheme of philosophic completeness. The thinkers did not seriously make any effort after this completeness. The Encyclopædia was the most serious attempt, and it did not wholly fail. As I replace in my shelves this mountain of volumes, "dusky and huge, enlarging on the sight," I have a presentiment that their pages will seldom again be disturbed by me or by others. They served a great purpose a hundred years ago. They are now a monumental ruin, clothed with all the profuse associations of history. It is no Ozymandias of Egypt, king of kings, whose wrecked shape of stone and sterile memories we contemplate. We think rather of the grey and crumbling walls of an ancient stronghold, reared by the endeavour of stout hands and faithful, whence in its own day and generation a band once went forth against barbarous hordes, to strike a blow for humanity and truth.'[1]

It is gratifying to find that the same view of the work of these famous men, and of its relation to the social necessities of the time, commends itself to Mr. Lecky, who has since gone diligently and with a candid mind over the same ground.[2] Then where is the literary Jacobin?

Of course, it is easy enough to fish out a sentence or a short passage here and there that, if taken by itself, may wear a sinister look, and carry alarming impressions. Not many days ago a writer addressed a letter to *The Times* that furnishes a specimen of this kind of controversy. He gave himself the ambiguous designation of 'Catholicus'; but his style bore traces of the equivocally Catholic climate of Munich. His aim was the lofty and magnanimous

[1] *Diderot*, i. 221-222.   [2] See his vol. vi. 305 *et seq*.

one of importing theological prejudice into the chief political dispute of the day; in the interest, strange to say, of the Irish party, who have been for ages the relentless oppressors of the Church to which he belongs, and who even now hate and despise it with all the virulence of a Parisian Red. This masked assailant conveys to the mind of the reader that I applaud and sympathise with the events of the winter of 1793, and more particularly with the odious procession of the Goddess of Reason at Notre Dame. He says, moreover, that I have 'the effrontery to imply that the horrible massacres of the Revolution . . . were "a very mild story compared with the atrocities of the Jews or the crimes of Catholicism."' No really honest and competent disputant would have hit on 'effrontery' as the note of the passage referred to, if he had had its whole spirit and drift before him. The reader shall, if he pleases, judge for himself. After the words just quoted, I go on to say:

'Historical recriminations, however, are not very edifying. It is perfectly fair, when Catholics talk of the atheist Terror, to rejoin that the retainers of Anjou and Montpensier slew more men and women on the first day of the Saint Bartholomew, than perished in Paris through the Years I. and II. of the Republic. But the retort does us no good beyond the region of dialectic. Some of the opinions of Chaumette were full of enlightenment and hope. But it would be far better to share the superstitious opinions of a virtuous and benignant priest, like the

Bishop in Victor Hugo's *Misérables*, than to hold those opinions of Chaumette, as he held them, with a rancorous intolerance, a reckless disregard of the rights and feelings of others, and a shallow forgetfulness of all that great and precious part of our nature that lies out of the immediate domain of the logical understanding. . . . In every family where a mother sought to have her child baptized, or where sons and daughters sought to have the dying spirit of the old consoled by the last sacrament, there sprang up a bitter enemy to the government that had closed the churches and proscribed the priests. How could a society whose spiritual life had been nourished in the solemn mysticism of the Middle Ages suddenly turn to embrace a gaudy paganism? The common self-respect of humanity was outraged by apostate priests . . . as they filed before the Convention, led by the Archbishop of Paris, and accompanied by rude acolytes bearing piles of the robes and the vessels of silver and gold with which they had once served their holy offices.'[1]

Where is the effrontery, the search for methods in the Reign of Terror, the applause for revolutionary models? Such inexcusable perversion of a writer's meaning for an evanescent political object is enough to make one think that George III. knew what he was talking about, when he once delivered himself of the saying that 'Politics are a trade for a rascal, not for a gentleman.'

[1] *Biog. Studies*, pp. 316, 317.

Let me cite another more grotesque piece of irrelevancy with a similar drift. Some months ago the present writer chanced to express an opinion upon Welsh Disestablishment. Wales, at any rate, would seem to be far enough away from *Émile, Candide,* the Law of Prairial, and the Committee of Public Safety. *The Times,* however, instantly said [1] that it would be affectation to express any surprise, because my unfortunate 'theories and principles, drawn from French sources and framed on French models, all tend to the disintegration of comprehensive political organisations and the encouragement of arrangements based on the minor peculiarities of race or dialect.' Was there ever in the world such prodigious nonsense? What French sources, what French models? If French models point in any one direction rather than another, it is away from disintegration and straight towards centralisation. Everybody knows that this is one of the most notorious facts of French history from the days of Louis XI. or Cardinal Richelieu down to Napoleon Bonaparte. So far from French models encouraging 'arrangements based on the minor peculiarities of race and dialect,' France is the first great example in modern history, for good or for evil, of a persevering process of national unification, and the firm suppression of all provincial particularismus. This is not only true of French political leaders in general: it is particularly true of the Jacobin leaders. Rousseau himself, I admit,

[1] Nov. 3, 1886.

did in one place point in the direction of confederation;
but only in the sense that for freedom on the one
hand, and just administration on the other, the unit
should not be too large to admit of the participation
of the persons concerned in the management of their
own public affairs. If the Jacobins had not been
overwhelmed by the necessity of keeping out the
invaders, they might have developed the germ of truth
in Rousseau's loose way of stating the expediency
of decentralisation. As it was, above all other
French schools, the Jacobins dealt most sternly with
particularist pretensions. Of all men, these supposed
masters, teachers, and models of mine are least to be
called Separatists. To them more than to any other
of the revolutionary parties the high-flying heresy of
Federalism was most odious; and if I were a faithful
follower of the Jacobin model, I should have least
patience with nationalist sentiment whether in Ireland, Scotland, or Wales, and should most rigorously
insist on that cast-iron incorporation which, as it
happens, in the case of Ireland I believe to be
equally hopeless and undesirable. This explanation,
therefore, of my favour for Welsh Disestablishment
is as absurdly ignorant as it is far-fetched and
irrelevant.

The logical process is worth an instant's examination. The position is no less than this,—that to
attempt truly to appreciate the place and the value
in the history of thought and social movements of
men who have been a hundred years in their graves,

and to sympathise with certain sides and certain effects of their activity under the peculiar circumstances in which French society then found itself, is the same thing as binding yourself to apply their theories and to imitate their activity, under an entirely heterogeneous set of circumstances, in a different country, and in a society with wholly dissimilar requirements. That is the argument, if we straighten it out. The childishness of any such contention is so obvious that I should be ashamed of reproducing it, were it not that this very contention has made its appearance at my expense several times a month for the last two years in all sorts of important and respectable prints.

For instance, it appears that I once said somewhere that Danton looked on at the doings of his bloodier associates with 'sombre acquiescence.' *Argal*, it was promptly pointed out—and I espy the dark phrase constantly adorning leading articles to this day—the man who said that Danton sombrely acquiesced in the doings of Billaud, Collot, and the rest, must of necessity, being of a firm and logical mind, himself sombrely acquiesce in moonlighting and cattle-houghing in Ireland. Apart from the curious compulsion of the reasoning, what is the actual state of the case? Acquiescence is hardly a good description of the mood of a politician who scorns delights and lives laborious days in actively fighting for a vigorous policy and an effective plan that, as he believes, would found order in Ireland on a new and more hopeful base. He may be wrong, but where is the acquiescence, sombre or serene?

The equally misplaced name of Fatalism is sometimes substituted for acquiescence, in criticisms of this stamp. In any such sense anybody is a fatalist who believes in a relation between cause and effect. If it is fatalism to assume that, given a certain chain of social or political antecedents, they will inevitably be followed by a certain chain of consequences, then every sensible observer of any series of events is a fatalist. Catholic Emancipation, the extension of the franchise, and secret ballot, have within the last sixty years completely shifted the balance of political power in Ireland. Land legislation has revolutionised the conditions of ownership. These vast and vital changes in Ireland have been accompanied by the transfer of decisive power from aristocracy to numbers in Great Britain, and Great Britain is arbiter. Is it fatalism, or is it only common sense, to perceive that one new effect of new causes so potent must be the necessity of changing the system of Irish government? To dream that you could destroy the power of the old masters without finding new, and that having invited the nation to speak you could continue to ignore the national sentiment was, and is, the very height of political folly, and the longer the dream is persisted in the ruder will be the awakening. Surely the stupidest fatalism is far more truly to be ascribed to those who insist that Ireland was eternally predestined to turmoil, confusion, and torment; that there alone the event defies calculation; and that, however wisely, carefully and providently you modify or extinguish causes, in Ireland, though nowhere else, effects will still survive with unaltered shape and unabated force.

No author has a right to assume that anybody has read all his books or any of them, but he may reasonably claim that he shall not be publicly classified, labelled, catalogued, and placed in the shelves, on the strength of half of his work, and that half arbitrarily selected. If it be permitted to me without excess of egotism to name the masters to whom I went to school in the days of early manhood, so far from being revolutionists and terrorists, they belonged entirely to the opposite camp. Austin's *Jurisprudence* and Mill's *Logic* and *Utilitarianism* were everything, and Rousseau's *Social Contract* was nothing. To the best of my knowledge and belief, I never said a word about 'Natural Rights' in any piece of practical public business in all my life; and when that famous phrase again made its naked appearance on the platform three or four years ago, it gave me as much surprise and dismay as if I were this afternoon to meet a deinotherium shambling down Parliament Street. Mill was the chief influence for me, as he was for most of my contemporaries in those days. Experience of life and independent use of one's mind—which he would have been the most ready of men to applaud—have since, as is natural, led to many important corrections and deductions in Mill's political and philosophical teaching. But then we were disciples, and not critics; and nobody will suppose that the devotee of Wordsworth, the author of the essay on Coleridge, and of the treatise on Representative Government, the administrator in the most bureaucratic and authoritative of public services, was a terrorist or an unbridled democrat, or anything else but the most careful and rationalistic of political theorisers. It was Mill who first held up for my admiration the illustrious man whom Austin enthusiastically called the ' godlike Turgot,' and it was he who encouraged me to write a study on that great and inspiring character. I remember the suspicion and the murmurings with which Louis Blanc, then living in brave and honourable exile in London, and the good friend of so many of us, who was really a literary Jacobin to the tips of his fingers, remonstrated against that piece of what he thought grievously misplaced glorification. Turgot was, indeed, a very singular hero with whom to open the career of literary Jacobin. So most assuredly was Burke, the most majestic of them all—the author of those wise sentences that still ring in our ears : ' *The question with me is, not whether you have a right to render your people miserable, but whether it is not your interest to make them happy. It is not what a lawyer tells me I may do, but what humanity, reason, and justice tell me I ought to do. Nobody shall persuade me, where a whole people are concerned, that acts of lenity are not means of conciliation.*' Burke, Austin, Mill, Turgot, Comte—

what strange sponsors for the 'theories and principles of the Terror'!

What these opinions came to, roughly speaking, was something to this effect: That the power alike of statesmen and of publicists over the course of affairs is strictly limited; that institutions and movements are not capable of immediate or indefinite modification by any amount of mere will; that political truths are always relative, and never absolute; that the test of practical, political, and social proposals is not their conformity to abstract ideals, but to convenience, utility, expediency, and occasion; that for the reformer, considerations of time and place may be paramount; and finally, as Mill himself has put it, that government is always either in the hands, or passing into the hands, of whatever is the strongest power in society, and that what this power is, and shall be, depends less on institutions than institutions depend upon it. If I were pressed for an illustration of these principles at work, inspiring the minds and guiding the practice of responsible statesmen in great transactions of our own day and generation, I should point to the sage, the patient, the triumphant action of Abraham Lincoln in the emancipation of the negro slaves. However that may be, contrast a creed of this kind with the abstract, absolute, geometric, unhistoric, peremptory notions and reasonings that formed the stock-in-trade of most, though not quite all, of the French revolutionists, alike in action and in thought. It is plain that they are the direct opposite and contradictory of one another.

To clench the matter by chapter and verse, I should like to recall what I have said of these theories and principles in their most perfect and most important literary version. How have I described Rousseau's *Social Contract*? It placed, I said, the centre of social activity elsewhere than in careful and rational examination of social conditions, and careful and rational effort to modify them. It substituted a retrograde aspiration for direction, and emotion for the discovery of law. It overlooked the crucial difficulty—namely, how to summon new force, without destroying the sound parts of a structure which it has taken many generations to erect. Its method was geometric instead of being historic, and hence its 'desperate absurdity.' Its whole theory was constructed with an imperfect consideration of the qualities of human nature, and with too narrow a view of human society. It ignored the master fact that government is the art of wisely dealing with huge groups of conflicting interests, of hostile passions, of hardly reconcilable aims, of vehemently opposed forces. It 'gives us not the least help towards the solution of any of the problems of actual government.'

Such language as all this is hardly that of a disciple to a master, in respect of theories and principles he is making his own for the use of a lifetime. ' There has been no attempt ' [in these pages], I said in winding up, ' to palliate either the shallowness or the practical mischievousness of the *Social Contract*. But there is another side to its influence. We should be false to our critical principle, if we do not recognise the historical effect of a speculation scientifically valueless.' Any writer would have stamped himself as both unfit for the task that I had undertaken, and entirely below the level of the highest critical standard of the day, if he had for a moment dreamed of taking any other point of view.

As for historical hero-worship, after Carlyle's fashion, whether with Jacobin idols or any other, it is a mood of mind that must be uncongenial to anybody who had ever been at all under the influence of Mill. Without being so foolish as to disparage the part played by great men in great crises, we could have no sympathy with the barbaric and cynical school, who make greatness identical with violence, force, and mere iron will. Cromwell said, in vindication of himself, that England had need of a constable, and it was true. The constable, the soldier, the daring counsellor at the helm, are often necessities of the time. It is often a necessity of the time that the energy of a nation or of a movement should gather itself up in a resolute band or a resolute chief; as the revolutionary energy of France gathered itself up in the greater Jacobins, or that of England in Oliver Cromwell. Goethe says that nature bids us ' *Take all, but pay.*' Revolutions and heroes may give us all, but not without price. This is at the best, and the best is the

A FEW WORDS ON FRENCH MODELS.

exception. The grandiose types mostly fail. In our own day, for example, people talk with admiration of Cromwell's government in Ireland—as if it were a success, instead of being one of the worst chapters in the whole crushing history of Irish failure. It was force carried to its utmost. Hundreds were put to the sword, thousands were banished to be slaves of the planters in the West Indies, and the remnant were driven miserably off into the desolate wilds of Connaught. But all this only prepared the way for further convulsions and deadlier discontent.

It is irrational to contrast Carlyle's heroes, Cromwell, Mirabeau, Frederick, Napoleon, with men like Washington or Lincoln. The circumstances were different. The conditions of public use and of personal greatness were different. But if we are to talk of ideals, heroes, and models, I, for one, should hardly look to France at all. Jefferson was no flatterer of George Washington, but his character of Washington comes far nearer to the right pattern of a great ruler than can be found in any of Carlyle's splendid dithyrambs, and it is no waste of time to recall and to transcribe it:

His mind was great and powerful, without being of the very first order; his penetration strong, though not so acute as that of a Newton, Bacon, or Locke; and as far as he saw, no judgment was ever sounder. It was slow in operation, being little aided by invention or imagination, but sure in conclusion. Hence the common remark of his officers, of the advantage he derived from councils of war, where, hearing all suggestions, he selected whatever was best: and certainly no general ever planned his battles more judiciously. But if deranged during the course of the action, if any member of his plan was dislocated by sudden circumstances, he was slow in a readjustment. He was incapable of fear, meeting personal dangers with the calmest unconcern. Perhaps the strongest feature in his character was prudence, never acting until every circumstance, every consideration, was maturely weighed; refraining if he saw a doubt, but when once decided, going through with his purpose, whatever obstacles opposed. His integrity was most pure, his justice the most inflexible I have ever known ; no motives of interest or consanguinity, of friendship or hatred, being able to bias his decision. He was, indeed, in every sense of the word, a wise, a good, and a great man. His temper was naturally irritable and high-toned; but reflection and resolution had obtained a firm and habitual ascendancy over it.

In conclusion, the plain truth is that all parallels, analogies, and similitudes between the French Revolution, or any part or phase of it, and our affairs in Ireland are moonshine. For the practical politician his problem is always individual. For his purposes history never repeats itself. Human nature doubtless has a weakness for a precedent; it is a weakness to be respected. But there is no such thing as an essential reproduction of social and political combinations of circumstance. To talk about Robespierre in connection with Ireland is just as idle as it was in Robespierre to harangue about Lycurgus and Brutus in Paris. To compare the two is to place Ireland under a preposterous magnifying-glass of monstrous dimension. Nor is disparity of scale the only difference, vital as that is. In no one of the leading characteristics of a community in a state of ferment, save the odium that surrounds the landlords, and that not universal, does Ireland to-day really resemble the France of a hundred years ago. Manners, ideas, beliefs, traditions, crumbling institutions, rising aspirations, the ordering of castes and classes, the rivalry of creeds, the relations with the governing power—all constitute elements of such radical divergence as to make comparison between modern Ireland and revolutionary France for any more serious purpose than giving a conventional and familiar point to a sentence, entirely worthless.

It is pure dilettantism, again, to seek the moral of Irish commotions in the insurrection of La Vendée. That, as somebody has said, was like a rising of the ancient Gauls at the voice of the Druids, and led by their great chiefs. It will be time enough to compare La Vendée with Ireland when the peasantry take the field against the British Government with Beresfords, Fitzgeralds, and Bourkes at their head. If the Vendéans had risen to drive out the Charettes, the Bonchamps, the Larochejacquelins, the parallel would have been nearer the mark. The report of the Devon Commission, the green pamphlet containing an account of the famous three days' discussion between O'Connell and Butt in the Dublin Corporation in 1843, or half a dozen of Lord Clare's speeches between 1793 and 1800, will give a clearer insight into the Irish problem than a bushel of books about the Vendéan or any other episode of the Revolution.

Equally frivolous is it, for any useful purpose of practical enlightenment, to draw parallels between the action of the Catholic clergy in Ireland to-day and that of the French clergy on the eve of the Revolution. There is no sort of force in the argument that because the French clergy fared ill at the Revolution,[1] therefore the Irish clergy will fare ill when self-government is bestowed on Ireland. Such talk is mere ingenious guess-work at best, without any of the foundations of a true historical analogy. The differences between the two cases are obvious, and they go to the heart of the matter. For instance, the men who came to the top of affairs in France were saturated both with speculative unbelief for one thing, and with active hatred of the Church for another. In Ireland, on the contrary, there is no speculative unbelief, as O'Connell used so constantly to boast; and the Church being poor, voluntary, and intensely national and popular, has nourished none of those gross and swollen abuses that provoked the not unreasonable animosity of revolutionary France. In truth, it is with precisely as much or as little reason that most of the soothsayers and prognosticators of evil take the directly

[1] The Church did not fare so very ill, after all. The State, in 1790, undertook the debts of the Church to the tune of 130,000,000 livres, and assured it an annual Budget of rather more than that amount (Boiteau's *État de la France*, p. 202).

opposite line. Instead of France these persons choose, as they have an equally good right to do, to look for precedents to Spain, Belgium, or South America. Why not? They assure us, in their jingle, that Home Rule means Rome Rule, that the priests will be the masters, and that Irish autonomy is only another name for the reign of bigotry, superstition, and obscurantism. One of these two mutually destructive predictions has just as much to say for itself as the other, and no more. We may leave the prophets to fight it out between them while we attend to our business, and examine facts and probabilities as they are, without the aid of capriciously adopted precedents and fantastical analogies.

Parallels from France, or anywhere else, may supply literary amusement; they may furnish a weapon in the play of controversy. They shed no light and do no service as we confront the solid facts of the business to be done. Louis the Fourteenth was the author of a very useful and superior commonplace when he wrote: 'No man who is badly informed can avoid reasoning badly. I believe that whoever is rightly instructed, and rightly persuaded of *all the facts*, would never do anything else but what he ought.' Another great French ruler, who, even more than Louis, had a piercing eye for men and the world of action, said that the mind of a general ought to be like a field-glass, and as clear; to see things exactly as they are, *et jamais se faire des tableaux*,—never to compose the objects before him into pictures. The same maxim is nearly as good for the man who has to conquer difficulties in the field of government; and analogies and parallels are one way of substituting pictures for plans and charts. The statesman's problem is individual. I am not so graceless as to depreciate history or literature either for public or for private persons. 'You are a man,' Napoleon said to Goethe; and there is no reason why literature should prevent the reader of books from being a man; why it should blind him to the great practical truths that the end of life is not to think but to will; that everything in the world has its decisive moment, which statesmen know and seize; that the genius of politics, as a great man of letters truly wrote, has not 'All or Nothing' for its motto, but seeks on the contrary to extract the greatest advantage from situations the most compromised, and never flings the helve after the hatchet. Like literature, the use of history in politics is to refresh, to open, to make the mind generous and hospitable; to enrich, to impart flexibility, to quicken and nourish political imagination and invention, to instruct in the common difficulties and the various experiences of government; to enable a statesman to place himself at a general and spacious standpoint. All this, whether it be worth much or little, and it is surely worth much, is something wholly distinct from directly aiding a statesman in the performance of a specific task. In such a case an analogy from history, if he be not sharply on his guard, is actually more likely than not to mislead him. I certainly do not mean the history of the special problem itself. Of that he cannot possibly know too much, nor master its past course and foregone bearings too thoroughly. Ireland is a great standing instance. There is no more striking example of the disastrous results of trying to overcome political difficulties without knowing how they came into existence, and where they have their roots. The only history that furnishes a clue in Irish questions is the history of Ireland and the people who have lived in it, or have been driven out of it.

AUGUSTE COMTE.[1]

COMTE is now generally admitted to have been the most eminent and important of that interesting group of thinkers whom the overthrow of old institutions in France turned towards social speculation. Vastly superior as he was to men like De Maistre on the one hand, and to men like Saint-Simon or Fourier on the other, as well in scientific acquisitions as in mental capacity, still the aim and interest of all his thinking was also theirs, namely, the renovation of the conditions of the social union. If, however, we classify him, not thus according to aim, but according to method, then he takes rank among men of a very different type from these. What distinguishes him in method from his contemporaries is his discernment that the social order cannot be transformed until all the theoretic conceptions belonging to it have been rehandled in a scientific spirit, and maturely gathered up into a systematic whole along with the rest of our knowledge. This presiding doctrine connects Comte with the social thinkers of the eighteenth

[1] Reprinted by the kind permission of Messrs. A. and C. Black from the ninth edition of the *Encyclopædia Britannica*.

century,—indirectly with Montesquieu, directly with Turgot, and more closely than either with Condorcet, of whom he was accustomed to speak as his philosophic father.

Isidore-Auguste-Marie-François-Xavier Comte was born in January 1798, at Montpellier, where his father was a receiver-general of taxes for the district. He was sent for his earliest instruction to the school of the town, and in 1814 was admitted to the École Polytechnique. His youth was marked by a constant willingness to rebel against merely official authority; to genuine excellence, whether moral or intellectual, he was always ready to pay unbounded deference. The strenuous application that was one of his most remarkable gifts in manhood showed itself in his youth, and his application was backed or inspired by superior intelligence and aptness. After he had been two years at the École Polytechnique he took a foremost part in a mutinous demonstration against one of the masters; the school was broken up, and Comte like the other scholars was sent home. To the great dissatisfaction of his parents, he resolved to return to Paris (1816), and to earn his living there by giving lessons in mathematics. Benjamin Franklin was the youth's idol at this moment. 'I seek to imitate the modern Socrates,' he wrote to a school friend, 'not in talents, but in way of living. You know that at five-and-twenty he formed the design of becoming perfectly wise, and that he fulfilled his design. I have dared to undertake the same thing, though I am not yet twenty.' Though Comte's character and aims were as far removed as possible from Franklin's type, neither Franklin nor any man that ever lived could surpass him in the heroic tenacity with which, in the face of a thousand obstacles, he pursued his own ideal of a vocation.

For a moment circumstances led him to think of seeking a career in America, but a friend who preceded him thither warned him of the purely practical spirit that prevailed in the new country. 'If Lagrange were to come to the United States, he could only earn his livelihood by turning land surveyor.' So Comte remained in Paris, living as he best could on something less than £80 a year, and hoping, when he took the trouble to break his meditations upon greater things by hopes about himself, that he might by and by obtain an appointment as mathematical master in a school. A friend procured him a situation as tutor in the house of Casimir-Périer. The salary was good, but the duties were too miscellaneous, and what was still worse, there was an end of the delicious liberty of the garret. After a short experience of three weeks Comte returned to neediness and contentment. He was not altogether without the young man's appetite for pleasure; yet when he was only nineteen we find him wondering, amid the gaieties of the carnival of 1817, how a gavotte or a minuet could make people forget that thirty thousand human beings around them had barely a morsel to eat. Hardship in youth has many drawbacks, but it has the immense advantage over academic ease of making the student's interest in men real, and not purely literary.

Towards 1818 Comte became associated as friend and disciple with a man who was destined to exercise a very decisive influence upon the turn of his speculation. Henry, Count of Saint-Simon, was second cousin of the famous Duke of Saint-Simon, the friend of the Regent, and author of the most important set of memoirs in a language that is so incomparably rich in memoirs. He was now nearly sixty, and if he had not gained a serious reputation, he had at least excited the curiosity and interest of his contemporaries by the social eccentricities of his life, by the multitude of his schemes and devices, and by the fantastic ingenuity of his political ideas. Saint-Simon's most characteristic faculty was an exuberant imagination, working in the sphere of real things. Scientific discipline did nothing for him; he had never undergone it, and he never felt its value. He was an artist in social construction; and if right ideas, or the suggestion of right ideas, sometimes came into his head, about history, about human progress, about a stable polity, such ideas were not the products of trains of ordered reasoning; they were the intuitional glimpses of the poet, and consequently as they professed to be in real matter, even the right ideas were as often as not accompanied by wrong ones.

The young Comte, now twenty, was enchanted by the philosophic veteran. In after years he so far forgot himself as to write of Saint-Simon as a depraved quack, and to deplore his connection with him as purely mischievous. While the connection lasted he thought very differently. Saint-Simon is described as the most estimable and lovable of men, and the most delightful in his relations; he is the worthiest of philosophers. Even after the association had come to an end, and at the very moment when Comte was congratulating himself on having thrown off the yoke, he honestly admits that Saint-Simon's influence has been of powerful service in his philosophic education. 'I certainly,' he writes to his most intimate friend, 'am under great personal obligations to Saint-Simon; that is to say, he helped in a powerful degree to launch me in the philosophical direction that I have now definitely marked out for myself, and that I shall follow without looking back for the rest of my life.' Even if there were no such unmistakable expressions as these, the most cursory glance into Saint-Simon's writings is enough to reveal the thread of connection between the ingenious visionary and the systematic thinker. We see the debt, and we also see that when it is stated at the highest possible, nothing has really been taken either from Comte's claims as a powerful original thinker, or from his immeasurable pre-eminence over Saint-Simon in intellectual grasp, vigour, and coherence. As high a degree of originality may be shown in transformation as in invention, as Molière and Shakespeare have proved in the region of dramatic art. In philosophy the conditions are not different. *Il faut prendre son bien où on le trouve.*

It is no detriment to Comte's fame that some of the ideas which he recombined and incorporated in a great philosophic structure had their origin in ideas produced almost at random in the incessant fermentation of Saint-Simon's brain. Comte is in no true sense a follower of Saint-Simon, but it was undoubtedly Saint-Simon who launched him, to take Comte's own word, by suggesting to his strong and penetrating mind the two starting-points of what grew into the Comtist system—first, that political phenomena are as capable of being grouped under laws as other phenomena; and second, that the true destination of philosophy must be social, and the true object of the thinker must be the reorganisation of the moral, religious, and political systems. We can readily see what an impulse these far-reaching conceptions would give to Comte's meditations. There were conceptions of less importance than these, in which it is impossible not to feel that it was Saint-Simon's wrong or imperfect idea that put his young admirer on the track to a right and perfected idea. The subject is not worthy of further discussion. That Comte would have performed some great intellectual achievement, if Saint-Simon had never been born, is certain. It is hardly less certain that the great achievement which he did actually perform was originally set in motion by Saint-Simon's conversation, though it was afterwards directly filiated with the fertile speculations of Turgot and Condorcet. Comte thought almost as meanly of Plato as he did of Saint-Simon, and he considered Aristotle the prince of all true thinkers; yet their vital difference about Ideas did not prevent Aristotle from calling Plato master.

After six years the differences between the old and the young philosopher grew too marked for friendship. Comte began to fret under Saint-Simon's pretensions to be his director. Saint-Simon, on the other hand, perhaps began to feel uncomfortably conscious of the superiority of his disciple. The occasion of the breach between them (1824) was an attempt on Saint-Simon's part to print a production of Comte's as if it were in some sort connected with Saint-Simon's schemes of social reorganisation. Comte was never a man to quarrel by halves, and not only was the breach not repaired, but long afterwards Comte, as we have said, with painful ungraciousness took to calling the encourager of his youth by very hard names.

In 1825 Comte married. His marriage was one of those of which 'magnanimity owes no account to prudence,' and it did not turn out prosperously. His family were strongly Catholic and royalist, and they were outraged by his refusal to have the marriage performed other than civilly. They consented, however, to receive his wife, and the pair went on a visit to Montpellier. Madame Comte conceived a dislike to the circle she found there, and this was the too early beginning of disputes which lasted for the remainder of their union. In the year of his marriage we find Comte writing to the most intimate of his correspondents:—'I have nothing left but to concentrate my whole moral existence in my intellectual work, a precious but inadequate compensation; and so I must give up, if not the most dazzling, still the sweetest part of my happiness.' We cannot help admiring the heroism that cherishes great ideas in the midst of petty miseries, and intrepidly throws all squalid interruptions into the background which is their true place. Still, we may well suppose that the sordid cares that come with want of money made a harmonious life none the more easy. Comte tried to find pupils to board with him, but only one pupil came, and he was soon sent away for lack of companions. 'I would rather spend an evening,' wrote the needy enthusiast, 'in solving a difficult question, than in running after some empty-headed and consequential millionaire in search of a pupil.' A little money was earned by an occasional article in *Le Producteur*, in which he began to expound the philosophic ideas that were now maturing in his mind. He announced a course of lectures (1826), that it was hoped would bring money as well as fame. They were to be the first dogmatic exposition of the Positive Philosophy. A friend had said to him, 'You talk too freely, your ideas are getting abroad, and other people use them without giving you the credit; put your ownership on record.' The lectures were intended to do this among other things, and they attracted hearers so eminent as Humboldt the cosmologist, Poinsot the geometer, Blainville the physiologist.

Unhappily, after the third lecture of the course, Comte had a severe attack of cerebral derangement, brought on by intense and prolonged meditation acting on a system already irritated by the chagrin of domestic failure. He did not recover his health for more than a year, and as soon as convalescence set in he was seized by so profound a melancholy at the disaster that had thus overtaken him, that he threw himself into the Seine. Fortunately he was rescued, and the shock did not stay his return to mental soundness. One incident of this painful episode is worth mentioning. Lamennais, then in the height of his Catholic exaltation, persuaded Comte's mother to insist on her son being married with the religious ceremony, and as the younger Madame Comte apparently did not resist, the rite was duly performed, in spite of the fact that the unfortunate man was at the time neither more nor less than raving mad. To such shocking conspiracies against common sense and decency does ecclesiastical zealotry bring even good men like Lamennais. On the other hand, philosophic assailants of Comtism have not always resisted the temptation to recall the circumstance that its founder was once out of his mind,— an unworthy and irrelevant device, that cannot be excused even by the provocation of Comte's own occasional acerbity. As has been justly said, if Newton once suffered a cerebral attack without on that account forfeiting our veneration for the *Principia*, Comte may have suffered in the same way, and still not have forfeited our respect for what is good in the systems of Positive Philosophy and Positive Polity.

In 1828 the lectures were renewed, and in 1830 was published the first volume of the *Course of Positive Philosophy*. The sketch and ground plan of this great undertaking had appeared in 1826. The sixth and last volume was published in 1842. The twelve years covering the publication of the first of Comte's two elaborate works were years of indefatigable toil, and they were the only portion of his life in which he enjoyed a certain measure, and that a very modest measure, of material prosperity. In 1833 he was appointed examiner of the boys in the various provincial schools who aspired to enter the École Polytechnique at Paris. This and two other engagements as a teacher of mathematics secured him an income of some £400 a year. He made M. Guizot, then Louis Philippe's minister, the important proposal to establish a chair of general history of the sciences. If there are four chairs, he argued, devoted to the history of philosophy, that is to say, the minute study of all sorts of dreams and aberrations through the ages, surely there ought to be at least one to explain the formation and progress of our real knowledge. This wise suggestion, which still remains to be acted upon, was at first welcomed, according to

Comte's own account, by Guizot's philosophic instinct, and then repulsed by his 'metaphysical rancour.'

Meanwhile Comte did his official work conscientiously, sorely as he grudged the time it took from the execution of the prime object of his thoughts. We cannot forbear to transcribe one delightful and touching trait in connection with this part of Comte's life. 'I hardly know if even to you,' he writes in the expansion of domestic confidence to his wife, ' I dare disclose the sweet and softened feeling that comes over me when I find a young man whose examination is thoroughly satisfactory. Yes, though you may smile, the emotion would easily stir me to tears if I were not carefully on my guard.' Such sympathy with youthful hope, in union with the industry and intelligence that are the only means of bringing the hope to fulfilment, shows that Comte's dry and austere manner veiled the fires of a generous social emotion. It was this that made the overworked student take upon himself the burden of delivering every year from 1831 to 1848 a course of gratuitous lectures on astronomy for a popular audience. The social feeling that inspired this disinterested act showed itself in other ways. He suffered the penalty of imprisonment rather than serve in the national guard; his position was that though he would not take arms against the new monarchy of July, yet being a republican he would take no oath to defend it. The only amusement that Comte permitted himself was a visit to the opera. In his youth he had been a playgoer, but he shortly came to the conclusion that tragedy is a stilted and bombastic art, and after a time comedy interested him no more than tragedy. For the opera he had a genuine passion, which he gratified as often as he could, until his means became too narrow to afford even that single relaxation.

Of his manner and personal appearance we have the following account from one who was his pupil:—
'Daily as the clock struck eight on the horologe of the Luxembourg, while the ringing hammer on the bell was yet audible, the door of my room opened, and there entered a man, short, rather stout, almost what one might call sleek, freshly shaven, without vestige of whisker or moustache. He was invariably dressed in a suit of the most spotless black, as if going to a dinner party; his white neckcloth was fresh from the laundress's hands, and his hat shining like a racer's coat. He advanced to the arm-chair prepared for him in the centre of the writing-table, laid his hat on the left-hand corner; his snuff-box was deposited on the same side beside the quire of paper placed in readiness for his use, and, dipping the pen twice into the ink-bottle, then bringing it to within an inch of his nose, to make sure it was properly filled, he broke silence: "We have said that the chord AB," etc. For three-quarters of an hour he continued his demonstration, making short notes as he went on, to guide the listener in repeating the problem alone; then, taking up another cahier which

lay beside him, he went over the written repetition of the former lesson. He explained, corrected, or commented till the clock struck nine; then, with the little finger of the right hand brushing from his coat and waistcoat the shower of superfluous snuff which had fallen on them, he pocketed his snuff-box, and resuming his hat, he as silently as when he came in made his exit by the door which I rushed to open for him.'

In 1842, as we have said, the last volume of the *Positive Philosophy* was given to the public. Instead of the contentment that we like to picture as the reward of twelve years of meritorious toil devoted to the erection of a high philosophic edifice, the author of this great contribution found himself in the midst of a very sea of small troubles. And they were troubles of the uncompensated kind that harass without elevating, and waste a man's spirit without softening or enlarging it. First, the jar of temperament between Comte and his wife had become so unbearable that they separated (1842). It is not expedient for strangers to attempt to allot blame in such cases, for it is impossible for strangers to know all the deciding circumstances. We need only say that in spite of one or two disadvantageous facts in her career that do not concern the public, Madame Comte seems to have uniformly comported herself towards her husband with an honourable solicitude for his well-being. Comte made her an annual allowance. and for some years after the separation they corresponded on friendly terms. Next in the list of the vexations that greeted Comte on emerging from the long tunnel of philosophising was a law-suit with his publisher. The publisher had impertinently inserted in the sixth volume a protest against a certain foot-note, in which Comte had used some hard words about M. Arago. Comte threw himself into the suit with an energy worthy of Voltaire, and he won it. Third, and worst of all, he had prefixed a preface to the sixth volume, in which he deliberately went out of his way to rouse the active enmity of the very men on whom depended his annual re-election to the post of examiner for the Polytechnic School. The result of this perversity was that by and by he lost the appointment, and with it one half of his very modest income. This was the occasion of an episode of more than merely personal interest.

Before 1842 Comte had been in correspondence with our distinguished countryman, J. S. Mill. Mill had been greatly impressed by Comte's philosophic ideas; he admits that his own *System of Logic* owes many valuable thoughts to Comte, and that, in the portion of that work which treats of the logic of the moral sciences, a radical improvement in the conceptions of logical method was derived from the *Positive Philosophy*. Their correspondence, which was extremely full and copious, and which we may hope will one day be made accessible to the public, turned principally upon the two great questions of the equality between men and women, and of the expediency and constitution of a sacerdotal or spiritual order. When Comte found himself straitened, he confided the entire circumstances to his English friend. As might be supposed by those who know the affectionate anxiety with which Mill regarded the welfare of any one whom he believed to be doing good work in the world, he at once took pains to have Comte's loss of income made up to him, until Comte should have had time to repair that loss by his own endeavour. Mill persuaded Grote, Molesworth, and Raikes Currie to advance the sum of £240. At the end of the year (that is, in 1845) Comte had taken no steps to enable himself to dispense with the aid of the three Englishmen. Mill applied to them again, but with the exception of Grote, who sent a small sum, they gave Comte to understand that they expected him to earn his own living. Mill had suggested to Comte that he should write articles for the English periodicals, and expressed his own willingness to translate any such articles from the French. Comte at first fell in with the plan, but he speedily surprised and disconcerted Mill by boldly taking up the position of 'high moral magistrate,' and accusing the three defaulting contributors of a scandalous falling away from righteousness and a high mind. Mill was chilled by these pretensions; they struck him as savouring of a totally unexpected charlatanry; and the correspondence came to an end. For Comte's position in the argument one feels that there is much to be said. If you have good reason for believing a given thinker to be doing work that will destroy the official system of science or philosophy, and if you desire its destruction, then you may fairly be asked to help to provide for him the same kind of material freedom that is secured to the professors and propagators of the official system by the State or by the universities. And if it is a fine thing for a man to leave money behind him in the shape of an endowment for the support of a scientific teacher of whom he has never heard, why should it not be just as natural and as laudable to give money, while he is yet alive, to a teacher whom he both knows and approves of? On the other hand, Grote and Molesworth might say that, for anything they could tell, they would find themselves to be helping the construction of a system of which they utterly disapproved. And, as things turned out, they would have been perfectly justified in this serious apprehension. To have done anything to make the production of the *Positive Polity* easier would have been no ground for anything but remorse to any of the three. It is just to Comte to remark that he always assumed that the contributors to the support of a thinker should be in all essentials of method and doctrine the thinker's disciples; aid from indifferent persons he counted irrational and humiliating. But is an endowment ever a blessing to the man who receives it? The question is difficult to answer generally; in Comte's case there is reason in the doubts felt by Madame Comte as to the expediency of relieving the philosopher from the necessity of being in plain and business-like relations with indifferent persons for a certain number of hours in the week. Such relations do as much as a doctrine to keep egoism within decent bounds, and they must be not only a relief, but a wholesome corrective to the tendencies of concentrated thinking on abstract subjects.

What finally happened was this. From 1845 to 1848 Comte lived as best he could, as well as made his wife her allowance, on an income of £200 a year. We need scarcely say that he was rigorously thrifty. His little account-books of income and outlay, with every item entered down to a few hours before his death, are accurate and neat enough to have satisfied an ancient Roman householder. In 1848, through no fault of his own, his salary was reduced to £80. M. Littré and others, with Comte's approval, published an appeal for subscriptions, and on the money thus contributed Comte subsisted for the remaining nine years of his life. By 1852 the subsidy produced as much as £200 a year. It is worth noticing, after the story we have told, that Mill was one of the subscribers, and that M. Littré continued his assistance after he had been driven from Comte's society by his high pontifical airs. We are sorry not to be able to record any similar trait of magnanimity on Comte's part. His character, admirable as it is for firmness, for intensity, for inexorable will, for iron devotion to what he thought the service of mankind, yet offers few of those softening qualities that make us love good men and pity bad ones. He is of the type of

Brutus or of Cato—a model of austere fixity of purpose, but ungracious, domineering, and not quite free from petty bitterness.

If you seek to place yourself in sympathy with Comte it is best to think of him only as the intellectual worker, pursuing in uncomforted obscurity the laborious and absorbing task to which he had given up his whole life. His singularly conscientious fashion of elaborating his ideas made the mental strain more intense than even so exhausting a work as the abstract exposition of the principles of positive science need have been, if he had followed a more self-indulgent plan. He did not write down a word until he had first composed the whole matter in his mind. When he had thoroughly meditated every sentence, he sat down to write, and then, such was the grip of his memory, the exact order of his thoughts came back to him as if without an effort, and he wrote down precisely what he had intended to write, without the aid of a note or a memorandum, and without check or pause. For example, he began and completed in about six weeks a chapter in the *Positive Philosophy* (vol. v. ch. lv.), which would fill forty of the large pages of the *Encyclopædia Britannica*. Even if his subject had been merely narrative or descriptive, this would be a very satisfactory piece of continuous production. When we reflect that the chapter in question is not narrative, but an abstract exposition of the guiding principles of the movements of several centuries, with many threads of complex thought running along side by side all through the speculation, then the circumstances under which it was reduced to literary form are really astonishing. It is hardly possible for a critic to share the admiration expressed by some of Comte's disciples for his style. We are not so unreasonable as to blame him for failing to make his pages picturesque or thrilling; we do not want sunsets and stars and roses and ecstasy; but there is a certain standard for the most serious and abstract subjects. When compared with such philosophic writing as Hume's, Diderot's, Berkeley's, then Comte's manner is heavy, laboured, monotonous, without relief and without light. There is now and then an energetic phrase, but as a whole the vocabulary is jejune; the sentences are overloaded; the pitch is flat. A scrupulous insistence on making his meaning clear led to an iteration of certain adjectives and adverbs, which at length deadens the effect beyond the endurance of all but the most resolute students. Only the profound and stimulating interest of much of the matter prevents one from thinking of Rivarol's ill-natured remark upon Condorcet, that he wrote with opium on a page of lead. The general effect is impressive, not by any virtues of style, for we do not discern one, but by reason of the magnitude and importance of the undertaking, and the visible conscientiousness and the grasp with which it is executed. It is by sheer strength of thought, by the vigorous perspicacity with which he strikes the lines of cleavage of his subject, that he makes his way into the mind of the reader; in the presence of gifts of this power we need not quarrel with an ungainly style.

Comte pursued one practice that ought to be mentioned in connection with his personal history, the practice of what he styled *hygiène cérébrale*. After he had acquired what he considered to be a sufficient stock of material, and this happened before he had completed the *Positive Philosophy*, he abstained deliberately and scrupulously from reading newspapers, reviews, scientific transactions, and everything else whatever, except two or three poets (notably Dante) and the *Imitatio Christi*. It is true that his friends kept him informed of what was going on in the scientific world. Still this partial divorce of himself from the record of the social and scientific activity of his time, though it may save a thinker from the deplorable evils of dispersion, moral and intellectual, accounts in no small measure for the exaggerated egoism, and the absence of all feeling for reality, which marked Comte's later days.

Only one important incident in Comte's life now remains to be spoken of. In 1845 he made the acquaintance of Madame Clotilde de Vaux, a lady whose husband had been sent to the galleys for life, and who was therefore, in all but the legal incidents of her position, a widow. Very little is known about her qualities. She wrote a little piece which Comte rated so preposterously as to talk about George Sand in the same sentence; it is in truth a flimsy performance, though it contains one or two gracious thoughts

There is true beauty in the saying—'*It is unworthy of a noble nature to diffuse its pain.*' Madame de Vaux's letters speak well for her good sense and good feeling, and it would have been better for Comte's later work if she had survived to exert a wholesome restraint on his exaltation. Their friendship had only lasted a year when she died (1846), but the period was long enough to give her memory a supreme ascendancy in Comte's mind. Condillac, Joubert, Mill, and other eminent men have shown what the intellectual ascendancy of a woman can be. Comte was as inconsolable after Madame de Vaux's death as D'Alembert after the death of Mademoiselle Lespinasse. Every Wednesday afternoon he made a reverential pilgrimage to her tomb, and three times every day he invoked her memory in words of passionate expansion. His disciples believe that in time the world will reverence Comte's sentiment about Clotilde de Vaux, as it reveres Dante's adoration of Beatrice—a parallel that Comte himself was the first to hit upon. It is no doubt the worst kind of cynicism to make a mock in a realistic vein of any personality that has set in motion the idealising thaumaturgy of the affections. Yet we cannot help feeling that it is a grotesque and unseemly anachronism to apply in grave prose, addressed to the whole world, those terms of saint and angel which are touching and in their place amid the trouble and passion of the great mystic poet. Only an energetic and beautiful imagination, together with a mastery of the rhythm and swell of impassioned speech, can prevent an invitation to the public to hearken to the raptures of intense personal attachment from seeming ludicrous and almost indecent. Whatever other gifts Comte may have had—and he had many of the rarest kind,—poetic imagination was not among them, any more than poetic or emotional expression was among them. His was one of those natures whose faculty of deep feeling is unhappily doomed to be inarticulate, and to pass away without the magic power of transmitting itself.

Comte lost no time, after the completion of his *Course of Positive Philosophy*, in proceeding with the *System of Positive Polity*, to which the earlier work was designed to be a foundation. The first volume was published in 1851, and the fourth and last in 1854. In 1848, when the political air was charged with stimulating elements, he founded the Positive Society, with the expectation that it might grow into a reunion as powerful over the new Revolution as the Jacobin Club had been in the Revolution of 1789. The hope was not fulfilled, but a certain number of philosophic disciples gathered round Comte, and eventually formed themselves, under the guidance of the new ideas of the latter half of his life, into a kind of church. In the years 1849, 1850, and 1851, Comte gave three courses of lectures at the Palais Royal. They were gratuitous and popular, and in them he boldly advanced the whole of his doctrine, as well as the direct and immediate pretensions of himself and his system. The third course ended in the following uncompromising terms—'In the name of the Past and of the Future, the servants of Humanity—both its philosophical and its practical servants — come forward to claim as their due the general direction of this world. Their object is to constitute at length a real Providence in all departments,—moral, intellectual, and material. Consequently they exclude once for all from political supremacy all the different servants of God—Catholic, Protestant, or Deist—as being at once behindhand and a cause of disturbance.' A few weeks after this invitation a very different person stepped forward to constitute himself a real Providence.

In 1852 Comte published the *Catechism of Positivism*. In the preface to it he took occasion to express his approval of Louis Napoleon's *coup d'état* of the 2nd of December,—'a fortunate crisis which has set aside the parliamentary system, and instituted a dictatorial republic.' Whatever we may think of the political sagacity of such a judgment, it is due to Comte to say that he did not expect to see his dictatorial republic transformed into a dynastic empire, and, next, that he did expect from the Man of December freedom of the press and of public meeting. His later hero was the Emperor Nicholas, 'the only statesman in Christendom,'—as unlucky a judgment as that which placed Dr. Francia in the Comtist Calendar.

In 1857 he was attacked by cancer, and died peaceably on the 5th of September of that year. The anniversary is always celebrated by ceremonial gatherings of his French and English followers, who then commemorate the name and the services of the founder of their religion. Comte was under sixty when he died. We cannot help reflecting that one of the worst of all the evils connected with the shortness of human life is the impatience it breeds in some of the most ardent and enlightened minds to hurry on the execution of projects, for which neither the time nor the spirit of their author is fully ripe.

In proceeding to give an outline of Comte's system, we shall consider the *Positive Polity* as the more or less legitimate sequel of the *Positive Philosophy*, notwithstanding the deep gulf which so eminent a critic as Mill insisted upon fixing between the earlier and the later work.[1] There may be, as we think

[1] The English reader is specially well placed for satisfying such curiosity as he may have about Comte's philosophy. Miss Martineau condensed the six volumes of the *Philosophie Positive* into two volumes of excellent English (1853); Comte himself gave them a place in the Positivist Library. The *Catechism* was translated by Dr. Congreve in 1858. The *Politique Positive* has been reproduced in English (Longmans, 1875-1877) by the conscientious labour of Comte's London followers. This translation is accompanied by a careful running analysis and explanatory summary of contents, that make the work more readily intelligible than the original. For criticisms, the reader may be referred to Mill's *Auguste Comte and Positivism*; Dr. Bridges's reply to Mill, *The Unity of Comte's Life and Doctrines* (1866); Herbert Spencer's essay on the *Genesis of Science*, and pamphlet on *The Classification of the Sciences*; Professor Huxley's 'Scientific Aspects of Positivism,' in his *Lay Sermons*; Dr. Congreve's *Essays Political, Social, and Religious* (1874); Fiske's *Outlines of Cosmic Philosophy* (1874); Lewes's *History of Philosophy*, vol. ii.

there is, the greatest difference in their value, and the temper is not the same, nor the method. But the two are quite capable of being regarded, and for the purposes of an account of Comte's career ought to be regarded, as an integral whole. His letters when he was a young man of one-and-twenty, and before he had published a word, show how strongly present the social motive was in his mind, and in what little account he should hold his scientific works, if he did not perpetually think of their utility for the species. 'I feel,' he wrote, 'that such scientific reputation as I might acquire would give more value, more weight, more useful influence to my political sermons.' In 1822 he published a *Plan of the Scientific Works necessary to reorganise Society*. In this opuscule he points out that modern society is passing through a great crisis, due to the conflict of two opposing movements,—the first, a disorganising movement owing to the break-up of old institutions and beliefs; the second, a movement towards a definite social state, in which all means of human prosperity will receive their most complete development and most direct application. How is this crisis to be dealt with? What are the undertakings necessary in order to pass successfully through it towards an organic state? The answer to this is that there are two series of works. The first is theoretic or spiritual, aiming at the development of a new principle of co-ordinating social relations and the formation of the system of general ideas that are destined to guide society. The second work is practical or temporal; it settles the distribution of power and the institutions that are most conformable to the spirit of the system that has previously been thought out in the course of the theoretic work. As the practical work depends on the conclusions of the theoretical, the latter must obviously come first in order of execution.

In 1826 this was pushed further in a remarkable piece called *Considerations on the Spiritual Power*— the main object of which is to demonstrate the necessity of instituting a spiritual power, distinct from the temporal power and independent of it. In examining the conditions of a spiritual power proper for modern times, he indicates in so many terms the presence in his mind of a direct analogy between his proposed spiritual power and the functions of the Catholic clergy at the time of its greatest vigour and most complete independence,—that is to say, from about the middle of the eleventh century until towards the end of the thirteenth. He refers to De Maistre's memorable book, *Du Pape*, as the most profound, accurate, and methodical account of the old spiritual organisation, and starts from that as the model to be adapted to the changed intellectual and social conditions of the modern time. In the *Positive Philosophy*, again (vol. v. p. 344), he distinctly says that Catholicism, reconstituted as a system on new intellectual foundations, would finally preside over the spiritual reorganisation of modern society. Much else could easily be quoted to the same effect. If unity of career, then, means that Comte from the beginning designed the institution of a spiritual power and the systematic reorganisation of life, it is difficult to deny him whatever credit that unity may be worth, and the credit is perhaps not particularly great. Even the re-adaptation of the Catholic system to a scientific doctrine was plainly in his mind thirty years before the final execution of the *Positive Polity*, though it is difficult to believe that he foresaw the religious mysticism in which the task was to land him. A great analysis was to precede a great synthesis, but it was the synthesis on which Comte's vision was centred from the first. Let us first sketch the nature of the analysis. Society is to be reorganised on the base of knowledge. What is the sum and significance of knowledge? That is the question which Comte's first master-work professes to answer.

The *Positive Philosophy* opens with the statement of a certain law, of which Comte was the discoverer, and which has always been treated both by disciples and dissidents as the key to his system. This is the Law of the Three States. It is as follows. Each of our leading conceptions, each branch of our knowledge, passes successively through three different phases; there are three different ways in which the human mind explains phenomena, each way following the other in order. These three stages are the Theological, the Metaphysical, and the Positive. Knowledge, or a branch of knowledge, is in the Theological state, when it supposes the phenomena under consideration to be due to immediate volition, either in the object or in some supernatural being. In the Metaphysical state, for volition is substituted abstract force residing in the object, yet existing independently of the object; the phenomena are viewed as if apart from the bodies manifesting them; and the properties of each substance have attributed to them an existence distinct from that substance. In the Positive state inherent volition, or external volition and inherent force or abstraction personified have both disappeared from men's minds, and the explanation of a phenomenon means a reference of it, by way of succession or resemblance, to some other phenomenon,—means the establishment of a relation between the given fact and some more general fact. In the Theological and Metaphysical state men seek a cause or an essence; in the Positive they are content with a law. To borrow an illustration from an able English disciple of Comte:—'Take the phenomenon of the sleep produced by opium. The Arabs are content to attribute it to the will of God. Molière's medical student accounts for it by a *soporific principle* contained in the opium. The modern physiologist knows that he cannot account for it at all. He can simply observe, analyse, and experiment upon the phenomena attending the action of the drug, and classify it with other agents analogous in character' (Dr. Bridges).

The first and greatest aim of the Positive Philosophy is to advance the study of society into the third of the three stages,—to remove social phenomena from the sphere of theological and metaphysical conceptions, and to introduce among them the same scientific observation of their laws that has given us physics, chemistry, physiology. Social physics will consist of the conditions and relations of the facts of society, and will have two departments,—one statical, containing the laws of order; the other dynamical, containing the laws of progress. While men's minds were in the theological state, political events, for example, were explained by the will of the gods, and political authority based on divine right. In the metaphysical state of mind, then, to retain our instance, political authority was based on the sovereignty of the people, and social facts were explained by the figment of a falling away from a state of nature. When the positive method has been finally extended to society, as it has been to chemistry and physiology, these social facts will be resolved, as their ultimate analysis, into relations with one another, and instead of seeking causes in the old sense of the word, men will only examine the conditions of social existence. When that stage has been reached, not merely the greater part, but the whole, of our knowledge will be impressed with one character—the character, namely, of positivity or scientificalness; and all our conceptions in every part of knowledge will be thoroughly homogeneous. The gains of such a change are enormous. The new philosophical unity will now in its turn regenerate all the elements that went to its own formation. The mind will pursue knowledge without the wasteful jar and friction of conflicting methods and mutually hostile conceptions; education will be regenerated; and society will reorganise itself on the only possible solid base—a homogeneous philosophy.

The *Positive Philosophy* has another object besides the demonstration of the necessity and propriety of a science of society. This object is to show the sciences as branches from a single trunk—is to give to science the ensemble or spirit of generality hitherto confined to philosophy, and to give to philosophy the rigour and solidity of science. Comte's special object is a study of social physics, a science that before his advent was still to be formed; his second object is a review of the methods and leading generalities of all the positive sciences already formed, so that we may know both what system of inquiry to follow in our new science, and also where the new science will stand in relation to other knowledge.

The first step in this direction is to arrange scientific method and positive knowledge in order, and this brings us to another cardinal element in the Comtist system, the classification of the sciences. In the front of the inquiry lies one main division, that, namely, between speculative and practical knowledge. With the latter we have no concern. Speculative or theoretic knowledge is divided into abstract and concrete. The former is concerned with the laws that regulate phenomena in all conceivable cases; the latter is concerned with the application of these laws

Concrete science relates to objects or beings; abstract science to events. The former is particular or descriptive; the latter is general. Thus, physiology is an abstract science; but zoology is concrete. Chemistry is abstract; mineralogy is concrete. It is the method and knowledge of the abstract sciences that the Positive Philosophy has to reorganise in a great whole.

Comte's principle of classification is, that the dependence and order of scientific study follows the dependence of the phenomena. Thus, as has been said, it represents both the objective dependence of the phenomena and the subjective dependence of our means of knowing them. The more particular and complex phenomena depend upon the simpler and more general. The latter are the more easy to study. Therefore science will begin with those attributes of objects that are most general, and pass on gradually to other attributes that are combined in greater complexity. Thus, too, each science rests on the truths of the sciences that precede it, while it adds to them the truths by which it is itself constituted. Comte's series or hierarchy is arranged as follows:—(1) Mathematics (that is, number, geometry, and mechanics), (2) Astronomy, (3) Physics, (4) Chemistry, (5) Biology, (6) Sociology. Each of the members of this series is one degree more special than the member before it, and depends upon the facts of all the members preceding it, and cannot be fully understood without them. It follows that the crowning science of the hierarchy, dealing with the phenomena of human society, will remain longest under the influence of theological dogmas and abstract figments, and will be the last to pass into the positive stage. You cannot discover the relations of the facts of human society without reference to the conditions of animal life; you cannot understand the conditions of animal life without the laws of chemistry; and so with the rest.

This arrangement of the sciences and the Law of the Three States are together explanatory of the course of human thought and knowledge. They are thus the double key of Comte's systematisation of the philosophy of all the sciences from mathematics to physiology, and his analysis of social evolution, which is the basis of sociology. Each science contributes its philosophy. The co-ordination of all these partial philosophies produces the general Positive Philosophy. 'Thousands had cultivated science, and with splendid success; not one had conceived the philosophy which the sciences, when organised, would naturally evolve. A few had seen the necessity of extending the scientific method to all inquiries, but no one had seen how this was to be effected. . . . The Positive Philosophy is novel as a philosophy, not as a collection of truths never before suspected. Its novelty is the organisation of existing elements. Its very principle implies the absorption of all that great thinkers had achieved; while incorporating their results it extended their methods. . . . What tradition brought was the results; what Comte brought was the organisation of these results. He always claimed to be the founder of the Positive Philosophy. That he had every right to such a title is demonstrable to all who distinguish between the positive sciences and the philosophy which co-ordinated the truths and methods of these sciences into a doctrine' (G. H. Lewes).

We may interrupt our short exposition here to remark that Comte's classification of the sciences has been subjected to a vigorous criticism by Herbert Spencer. Spencer's two chief points are these:— (1) He denies that the principle of the development of the sciences is the principle of decreasing generality; he asserts that there are as many examples of the advent of a science being determined by increasing generality as by increasing speciality. (2) He holds that any grouping of the sciences in a succession gives a radically wrong idea of their genesis and their interdependence; no true filiation exists; no science develops itself in isolation; no one is independent, either logically or historically. M. Littré, by far the most eminent of the scientific followers of Comte, concedes a certain force to Spencer's objections, and makes certain secondary modifications in the hierarchy in consequence, while still cherishing his faith in the Comtist theory of the sciences. Mill, while admitting the objections as good, if Comte's arrangement pretended to be the only one possible, still holds that arrangement as tenable for the purpose with which it was devised. Lewes asserts against Spencer that the arrangement in a series is necessary, on grounds similar to those which require that the various truths constituting a science should be systematically co-ordinated, although in nature the phenomena are intermingled.

The first three volumes of the *Positive Philosophy* contain an exposition of the partial philosophies of the five sciences that precede sociology in the hierarchy. Their value has usually been placed very low by the special followers of the sciences concerned; they say that the knowledge is second-hand, is not coherent, and is too confidently taken for final. The Comtist replies that the task is philosophic, and is not to be judged by the minute accuracies of science. In these three volumes Comte took the sciences roughly as he found them. His eminence as a man of science must be measured by his only original work in that department—the construction, namely, of the new science of society. This work is accomplished in the last three volumes of the *Positive Philosophy* and the second and third volumes of the *Positive Polity*. The Comtist maintains that even if these five volumes together fail in laying down correctly and finally the lines of the new science, still they are the first solution of a great problem hitherto unattempted. 'Modern biology has got beyond Aristotle's conception; but in the construction of the biological science, not even the most unphilosophical biologist would fail to recognise the value of Aristotle's attempt. So for sociology. Subsequent sociologists may have conceivably to remodel the whole science, yet not the less will they recognise the merit of the first work which has facilitated their labours' (Congreve).

We shall now briefly describe Comte's principal conceptions in sociology, his position in respect to which is held by himself, and by others, to raise him to the level of Descartes or Leibnitz. Of course the first step was to approach the phenomena of human character and social existence with the expectation of finding them as reducible to general laws as the other phenomena of the universe, and with the hope of exploring these laws by the same instruments of observation and verification as had done such triumphant work in the case of the latter. Comte separates the collective facts of society and history from the individual phenomena of biology; then he withdraws these collective facts from the region of external volition, and places them in the region of law. The facts of history must be explained, not by providential interventions, but by referring them to conditions inherent in the successive stages of social existence. This conception makes a science of society possible. What is the method? It comprises, besides observation and experiment (which is, in fact, only the observation of abnormal social states), a certain peculiarity of verification. We begin by deducing every well-known historical situation from the series of its antecedents. Thus we acquire a body of empirical generalisations as to social phenomena, and then we connect the generalisations with the positive theory of human nature. A sociological demonstration lies in the establishment of an accordance between the conclusions of historical analysis and the preparatory conceptions of biological theory. As Mill puts it:—'If a sociological theory, collected from historical evidence, contradicts the established general laws of human nature; if (to use Comte's instances) it implies, in the mass of mankind, any very decided natural bent, either in a good or in a bad direction; if it supposes that the reason, in average human beings, predominates over the desires or the disinterested desires over the personal,—we may know that history has been misinterpreted, and that the theory is false. On the other hand, if laws of social phenomena, empirically generalised from history, can, when once suggested, be affiliated to the known laws of human nature; if the direction actually taken by the developments and changes of human society can be seen to be such as the properties of man and of his dwelling-place made antecedently probable, the empirical generalisations are raised into positive laws, and sociology becomes a science.' The result of this method is an exhibition of the events of human experience in co-ordinated series that manifest their own graduated connection.

Next, as all investigation proceeds from that which is known best, to that which is unknown or less well known, and as, in social states, it is the collective phenomenon that is more easy of access to the observer than its parts, therefore we must consider and pursue all the elements of a given social state together and in common. The social organisation must be viewed and explored as a whole. There is a nexus between each leading group of social phenomena and other leading groups; if there is a change in one of them, that change is accompanied by a corresponding modification of all the rest. 'Not only must political institutions and social manners on the one hand, and manners and ideas on the other, be always mutually connected; but further, this consolidated whole must be always connected by its nature with the corresponding state of the integral development of humanity, considered in all its aspects of intellectual, moral and physical activity' (Comte).

Is there any one element which communicates the decisive impulse to all the rest,—any predominating agency in the course of social evolution? The answer is that all the other parts of social existence are associated with, and drawn along by, the contemporary condition of intellectual development. The Reason is the superior and preponderant element that settles the direction in which all the other faculties shall expand. 'It is only through the more and more marked influence of the reason over the general conduct of man and of society that the gradual march of our race has attained that regularity and persevering continuity which distinguish it so radically from the desultory and barren expansion of even the highest animal orders, which share, and with enhanced strength, the appetites, the passions, and even the primary sentiments of man.' The history of intellectual development, therefore, is the key to social evolution, and the key to the history of intellectual development is the Law of the Three States.

Among other central thoughts in Comte's explanation of history are these :—The displacement of theological by positive conceptions has been accompanied by a gradual rise of an industrial *régime* out of the military *régime* ;—the great permanent contribution of Catholicism was the separation it set up between the temporal and the spiritual powers ;—the progress of the race consists in the increasing preponderance of the distinctively human elements over the animal elements ;—the absolute tendency of ordinary social theories will be replaced by an unfailing adherence to the relative point of view, and from this it follows that the social state, regarded as a whole, has been as perfect in each period as the co-existing condition of humanity and its environment would allow.

The elaboration of those ideas in relation to the history of the civilisation of the most advanced portion of the human race occupies two of the volumes of the *Positive Philosophy*, and has been accepted by competent persons of very different schools as a masterpiece of rich, luminous, and far-reaching suggestion. Whatever additions it may receive, and whatever corrections it may require, this analysis of social evolution will continue to be regarded as one of the great achievements of human intellect. The demand for the first of Comte's two works has gone on increasing in a significant degree. It was completed, as we have said, in 1842. A second edition was published in 1864; a third some years afterwards; and while we write (1876) a fourth is in the press. Three editions within twelve years of a work of abstract philosophy in six considerable volumes are the measure of a very striking influence. On the whole, we may suspect that no part of Comte's works has had so much to do with this marked success as his survey and review of the course of history.

The third volume of the later work, the *Positive Polity*, treats of social dynamics, and takes us again over the ground of historic evolution. It abounds with remarks of extraordinary fertility and comprehensiveness; but it is often arbitrary; its views of the past are strained into coherence with the statical views of the preceding volume; and so far as concerns the period to which the present writer happens to have given special attention, it is usually slight and sometimes random. As it was composed in rather less than six months, and as the author honestly warns us that he has given all his attention to a more profound co-ordination, instead of working out the special explanations more fully, as he had promised, we need not be surprised if the result is disappointing to those who had mastered the corresponding portion of the *Positive Philosophy*. Comte explains the difference between his two works. In the first his 'chief object was to discover and demonstrate the laws of progress, and to exhibit in one unbroken sequence the collective destinies of mankind, till then invariably regarded as a series of events wholly beyond the reach of explanation, and almost depending on arbitrary will. The present work, on the contrary, is addressed to those who are already sufficiently convinced of the certain existence of social laws, and desire only to have them reduced to a true and conclusive system.'

What that system is it would take far more space than we can afford to sketch even in outline. All we can do is to enumerate some of its main positions. They are to be drawn not only from the *Positive Polity*, but from two other works,—the *Positivist Catechism: a Summary Exposition of the Universal Religion, in Twelve Dialogues between a Woman and a Priest of Humanity;* and second, *The Subjective Synthesis* (1856), which is the first and only volume of a work upon mathematics announced at the end of the *Positive Philosophy*. The system for which the *Positive Philosophy* is alleged to have been the scientific preparation contains a Polity and a Religion; a complete arrangement of life in all its aspects, giving a wider sphere to Intellect, Energy, and Feeling than could be found in any of the previous organic types,—Greek, Roman, or Catholic-feudal. Comte's immense superiority over such pre-Revolutionary utopians as the abbé Saint-Pierre, no less than over the group of post-Revolutionary utopians, is especially visible in his firm grasp of the cardinal truth that the improvement of the social organism can only be effected by a moral development, and never by any changes in mere political mechanism, or any violences in the way of an artificial redistribution of wealth. A moral transformation must precede any real advance. The aim, both in public and private life, is to secure to the utmost possible extent the victory of the social feeling over self-love, or Altruism over Egoism. This is the key to the regeneration of social existence, as it is the key to that unity of individual life that makes all our energies converge freely and without wasteful friction towards a common end. What are the instruments for securing the preponderance of Altruism? Clearly they must work from the strongest element in human nature, and this element is Feeling or the Heart. Under the Catholic system the supremacy of Feeling was abused, and the Intellect was made its slave. Then followed a revolt of Intellect against Sentiment. The business of the new system will be to bring back the Intellect into a condition, not of slavery, but of willing ministry to the Feelings. The subordination never was, and never will be, effected except by means of a religion, and a religion, to be final, must include a harmonious synthesis of all our conceptions of the external order of the universe. The characteristic basis of a religion is the existence of a Power without us, so superior to ourselves as to command the complete submission of our whole life. This basis is to be found in the Positive stage, in Humanity, past, present, and to come, conceived as the Great Being

A deeper study of the great universal order reveals tc us at length the ruling power within it of the true Great Being, whose destiny it is to bring that order continually to perfection by constantly conforming to its laws, and which thus best represents to us that system as a whole. This undeniable Providence, the supreme dispenser of our destinies, becomes in the natural course the common centre of our affections, our thoughts, and our actions. Although this Great Being evidently exceeds the utmost strength of any, even of any collective, human force, its necessary constitution and its peculiar function endow it with the truest sympathy towards all its servants. The least amongst us can and ought constantly to aspire to maintain and even to improve this Being. This natural object of all our activity, both public and private, determines the true general character of the rest of our existence, whether in feeling or in thought ; which must be devoted to love, and to know, in order rightly to serve, our Providence, by a wise use of all the means which it furnishes to us. Reciprocally this continued service, while strengthening our true unity, renders us at once both happier and better.

The exaltation of Humanity into the throne occupied by the Supreme Being under monotheistic systems made all the rest of Comte's construction easy enough. Utility remains the test of every institution, impulse, act ; his fabric becomes substantially an arch of utilitarian propositions, with an artificial Great Being inserted at the top to keep them in their place. The Comtist system is utilitarianism crowned by a fantastic decoration. Translated into the plainest English, the position is as follows: 'Society can only be regenerated by the greater subordination of politics to morals, by the moralisation of capital, by the renovation of the family, by a higher conception of marriage, and so on. These ends can only be reached by a heartier development of the sympathetic instincts. The sympathetic instincts can only be developed by the Religion of Humanity.' Looking at the problem in this way, even a moralist who does not expect theology to be the instrument of social revival, might still ask whether the sympathetic instincts will not necessarily be already developed to their highest point, before people will be persuaded to accept the religion that is at bottom hardly more than sympathy under a more imposing name. However that may be, the whole battle—into which we shall not enter—as to the legitimateness of Comtism as a religion turns upon this erection of Humanity into a Being. The various hypotheses, dogmas, proposals, as to the family, to capital, etc. are merely propositions measurable by considerations of utility and a balance of expediencies. Many of these proposals are of the highest interest, and many of them are actually available; but there does not seem to be one of them of an available kind that could not equally well be approached from other sides, and even incorporated in some radically antagonistic system. Adoption, for example, as a practice for improving the happiness of families and the welfare of society, is capable of being weighed, and can in truth only be weighed by utilitarian considerations, and has been commended by men to whom the Comtist religion is naught. The singularity of Comte's construction, and the test by which it must be tried, is the transfer of the worship and discipline of Catholicism to a system in which 'the conception of God is superseded' by the abstract idea of Humanity, conceived as a kind of Personality.

And when all is said, the invention does not help us. We have still to settle what *is* for the good of Humanity, and we can only do that in the old-fashioned way. There is no guidance in the conception. No effective unity can follow from it, because you can only find out the right and wrong of a given course by summing up the advantages and disadvantages, and striking a balance, and there is nothing in the Religion of Humanity to force two men to find the balance on the same side. The Comtists are no better off than other utilitarians in judging policy, events, conduct.

The particularities of the worship, its minute and truly ingenious re-adaptation of sacraments, prayers, reverent signs, down even to the invocation of a new Trinity, need not detain us. They are said, though it is not easy to believe, to have been elaborated by way of Utopia. If so, no Utopia has ever yet been presented in a style so little calculated to stir the imagination, to warm the feelings, to soothe the insurgency of the reason. It is a mistake to present a great body of hypotheses—if Comte meant them for hypotheses—in the most dogmatic and peremptory form to which language can lend itself. And there is no more extraordinary thing in the history of opinion than the perversity with which Comte has succeeded in clothing a philosophic doctrine, so intrinsically conciliatory as his, in a shape that excites so little sympathy and gives so much provocation. An enemy defined Comtism as Catholicism *minus* Christianity, to which an able champion retorted by calling it Catholicism *plus* Science. Hitherto Comte's Utopia has pleased the followers of the Catholic just as little as those of the scientific spirit.

The elaborate and minute systematisation of life, proper to the religion of Humanity, is to be directed by a priesthood. The priests are to possess neither wealth nor material power; they are not to command, but to counsel; their authority is to rest on persuasion, not on force. When religion has become positive and society industrial, then the influence of the Church upon the State becomes really free and independent, which was not the case in the Middle Age. The power of the priesthood rests upon special knowledge of man and nature; but to this intellectual eminence must also be added moral power and a certain greatness of character, without which force of intellect and completeness of attainment will not receive the confidence they ought to inspire. The functions of the priesthood are of this kind:—To exercise a systematic direction over education; to hold a consultative influence over all the important acts of actual life, public and private; to arbitrate in cases of practical conflict; to preach sermons recalling those principles of generality and universal harmony which our special activities dispose us to ignore; to order the due classification of society; to perform the various ceremonies appointed by the founder of the religion. The authority of the priesthood is to rest wholly on voluntary adhesion, and there is to be perfect freedom of speech and discussion; though, by the way, we cannot forget Comte's detestable congratulations to the Czar Nicholas on the 'wise vigilance' with which he kept watch over the importation of western books.

From his earliest manhood Comte had been powerfully impressed by the necessity of elevating the condition of women (see remarkable passage in his letters to M. Valat, pp. 84-87). His friendship with Madame de Vaux had deepened the impression, and in the reconstructed society women are to play a highly important part. They are to be carefully excluded from public action, but they are to do many more important things than things political. To fit them for their functions, they are to be raised above material cares, and they are to be thoroughly educated. The family, that is so important an element of the Comtist scheme of things, exists to carry the influence of woman over man to the highest point of cultivation. Through affection she purifies the activity of man. 'Superior in power of affection, more able to keep both the intellectual and the active powers in continual subordination to feeling, women are formed as the natural intermediaries between Humanity and man. The Great Being confides specially to them its moral Providence, maintaining through them the direct and constant cultivation of universal affection, in the midst of all the distractions of thought or action, which are for ever withdrawing men from its influence. . . . Beside the uniform influence of every woman on every man, to attach him to Humanity, such is the importance and the difficulty of this ministry, that each of us should be placed under the special guidance of one of these angels, to answer for him, as it were, to the Great Being. This moral guardianship may assume three types,—the mother, the wife, and the daughter; each having several modifications, as shown in the concluding volume. Together they form the three simple modes of solidarity, or unity with contemporaries,—obedience, union, and protection,—as well as the three degrees of continuity between ages, by uniting us with the past, the present, and the future. In accordance with my theory of the brain, each corresponds with one of our three altruistic instincts,—veneration, attachment, and benevolence.'

How the positive method of observation and verification of real facts has landed us in this, and much else of the same kind, is extremely hard to guess. Seriously to examine an encyclopædic system, that touches life, society, and knowledge at every point, is evidently beyond the compass of such an article as this. There is in every chapter a whole group of speculative suggestions, each of which would need a long chapter to itself to elaborate or to discuss. There is at least one biological speculation of astounding audacity that could be examined in nothing less than a treatise. Perhaps we have said enough to show that after performing a great and real service to thought, Comte almost sacrificed his claims to gratitude by the invention of a system that, as such, and independently of detached suggestions, is markedly retrograde. But the world has strong self-protecting qualities. It will take what is available in Comte, while forgetting in his work that which is as irrational in one way as Hegel is in another.

THE END

Printed in Great Britain by R. & R. CLARK, LIMITED, *Edinburgh*